Kieran Youens-Byrne

Survivor

By

Kieran Youens-Byrne

Copyright © 2023 Kieran Youens-Byrne

All rights reserved.

ISBN: 9798375288093

Kieran Youens-Byrne – Survivor

DEDICATION

Thank you, Antony, Emma, Kaye, Mark, Carol, Marcel, Mark 1, Mark 2, Andy, Tracy, Pete, Roddy, Katie, Andrea, Sanny, Onon, Danny, Mo, Shazza, Denise, Jeanie, Callum, Sean, Colin, Gary, Vance
You have all been a part of my journey and my recovery before, during and after Rehab.

To my family and close friends, thank you for getting me on the path I never knew I needed to be on, for your unconditional support and love throughout my journey.

To my Ex-Wife and my Narcissist, without you, fake promises of love and forever, I'd never been able to be me and be better. I really did have to let you lose me so I could love me. You taught me that maybe the parts of me you stole were not the parts of me that I wanted. Maybe you needed them parts of me. If they helped you. You are welcome to them.

To my best friend, my confidant, my secret therapist. To the person that showed me who I truly am on the inside. You are such and amazing person, Without you, I wouldn't be here now. I wouldn't be exceeding my potential. I wouldn't feel as good about myself as I do. You really did save my life.

To my forever, my partner, my happily ever after. The woman who taught me what your other half actually means. I know you was the last chapter in my story. I want us to be our last loves. I want to thank you for coming into my life so blindly, you are truly and whole heartedly there for me. You fixed the pieces of me I didn't know need fixing, You showed me love comes at no cost. It knows no limits and it asks for nothing but true reciprocation

CONTENTS

	Acknowledgments	i
	Playlist	Pg 1
1	Hello, My Name is Alcoholism	Pg 5
2	Quotes About Addiction and Treatment	Pg 8
3	A Letter To My Younger Self	Pg 24
4	Quotes on Love and Heartbreak	Pg 28
5	A Narcissist's Exposure	Pg 37
5b.	My Narcissist's Exposure	Pg 42
6	Quotes on Healing From Heartbreak	Pg 52

7	Four Weeks Before Rehab	Pg 68
8	What My Addiction Led Me To	Pg 76
9	Kieran's Story	Pg 96
10	Quotes on Rebuilding	Pg 110
11	Quotes about Falling in Love	Pg 148
12	Falling In Love for the Last Times	Pg 164
13	Local Treatment Services	Pg 171
14	The Disease Concept	Pg 174
	About The Author	Pg 191

Kieran Youens-Byrne – Survivor

ACKNOWLEDGMENTS

I wouldn't be alive now if it wasn't for all the amazing Nursing staff at
The Alcohol Care Team at the Royal Oldham Hospital, Not only did they save my life, but they taught me, finding the right Rehabilitation Centre is like finding your perfect cooked breakfast.
Thank you! Without your support in getting me sober and staying sober at the beginning of my journey to being clean and serene, I wouldn't be here today.

Special Thanks Also to,
Carol Hughes, Royal Oldham Hospital,
Chapman Barker Unit, Prestwich,
Alcoholic Anonymous, Ashton-Under-Lyne,
Holgate House, Nelson

PLAYLIST

1. *Heart of Stone – SIX The Musical*

A Song which really helped me through working out my feelings after the initial shock of being released from a Narcissist, swearing I'd never fall in love again.

2. *I'll Never Love Again – Lady Gaga*

A song which genuinely touched my feelings at the time. A realisation that I never wanted to kiss another stranger, to start a fire with someone else. To wanting to be alone. This was in a period of self-sabotage. One which I was made to feel Isolated and very alone.

3. *Objects In The Rear-view Mirror – Meatloaf*

I got the words from this song tattooed on me, I know the actual song is about offspring abuse, however I relate to it, as the death of my addict. Even though it could be a good day and a spectacular day I'm having I have to be reminded that my addiction could easily take over, especially if I don't follow the steps.

4. *Defying Gravity – Wicked The Musical*

Is a trueness a legible word? Because that's what this song is to me, it's uplifting and motivational. It's a harsh reminder, that I'm finally emotionally mature, that there isn't any way of holding me back.

5. *Fight Song – Rachel Platten*

A Song I heavily listened to after detox. Where I found that last ounce of fight in me, the one little bit that showed me there was enough left in me to kickstart my life again.

6. *All I know So Far – P!nk!*

I'm healing, adjusting and getting better. However, this song reminds me it's all I know so far, and I have a future, that I vow I will do anything to protect.

7. *Balance – Lucy Spraggan*

After starting therapy, this is a heart hitting song, which I listen to humbly remind me, nobody can recover on their own. No man is an island. That sometimes you have to go to the mainland. That I am fortunate to know I am weightless on my therapist's shoulders.

8. *I Am Here – P!nk*

There are no words! No words to express how uplifting this song is, especially if it captures you. When you realise that you're a different entity, That you've changed for the better.

9. *For Good – Wicked*

Finally. A goodbye to my narcissist, a thank you. For releasing me. Also, for the lesson your fake love taught, of the things I will not tolerate and will not have in my life. Because I knew you, I have been changed for good.

10. *Special Mention – Last Love – Jon Mullins*

Such a heart-warming song, played to me by my partner.

Who unapologetically played this to me, who captured me, in spirit, who showed me emotional vulnerability. Who showed me sometimes love works. Thank you,

11. Special Mention – Lose You To Love Me – Selina Gomez

An indiscreet final song by again my amazing partner. I said a week before I met her, I would be receiving in a major way.
She randomly played this song on a playlist. I listen to it now and it reminds me how I had to lose the old Kieran, How I had to regenerate.
It say we a lot. Like it was me and the addict doing things together. I'm glad I lost the addict.

1. HELLO, MY NAME IS ALCOHOLISM

Hello, my name is Alcoholism– I destroy homes, tear families apart, take your children, and that's just the start.

I'm more costly than diamonds, more costly than gold, the sorrow I bring is a sight to behold.

and if you need me, remember I'm easily found, I live all around you, in schools and in town.

I live with the rich, I live with the poor, I live down the street, and maybe next door.

My power is awesome; try me you'll see, but if you do, you may NEVER break free.

Just try me once and I might let you go, but try me twice, and I'll own your soul.

When I possess you, you'll lie. You do what you must just to get drunk.

The displeasure you'll cause, for my narcotic charms will be worth the pleasure you'll feel in your head

You'll lie to your wife. You'll hide from your dad. When you see their tears, you should feel bad.

But you'll forget your morals and how you were raised, I'll be your conscience, I'll teach you, my ways.

I take kids from parents, and parents from kids, I turn people from God, and separate friends.

I'll take everything from you, your looks and your pride, I'll be with you always, right by your side.

You'll give up everything… your family, your home… your friends, your money, then you'll be alone.

I'll take and take, till you have nothing more to give. When I'm finished with you, you'll be lucky to live.

If you try me be warned this is no game. If given the chance, I'll drive you insane.

I'll ravish your body; I'll control your mind. I'll own you completely; your soul will be mine.

The nightmares I'll give you while lying in bed, the voices you'll hear from inside your head,

the sweats, the shakes, the visions you'll see; I want you to know, these are all gifts from me,

But then it's too late, and you'll know in your heart, that you are mine, and we shall not part.

You'll regret that you tried me, they always do, but you came to me, not I to you.

You knew this would happen. Many times, you were told, but you challenged my power, and chose to be bold.

You could have said no, and just walked away, if you could live that day over, now what would you say?

I'll be your master; you will be my slave, I'll even go with you, when you go to your grave.

Now that you have met me, what will you do? Will you try me or not? It's all up to you.

I can bring you more misery than words can tell. Come take my hand, I'll take you to HELL!

2. QUOTES ABOUT TREATMENT AND ADDICTION

JUST FOR TODAY

Just for today I will trust, risk and share and in doing so I will recover.

TELL THEM

Tell them I was human.

Tell them that I tried.

Tell them that even on my darkest nights, I reached for the light with the last shred of hope that my spirit could hold.

When I am gone, tell them how I loved like the surface of the sun.

Tell them what I did when I was warm, and breathing, and perfectly imperfect.

CHOICES

I never chose to be an addict.

The powerful force of addiction chose me.

I heard the warnings. I saw the signs.

I had ignored them all. I saw my life…

I saw my life collapse before me.

OH FATHER

What did I put my old man through? I'd have forsaken this man, more than a time or two.

He watched me shake, sweat and vomit. No words could thank him. Not even in this Sonnet.

I could read rhyme and verse. If only I could remove from his mind, the image of a hearse.

For he saved his son and reunited him with his Mum.

Thank you, Father and Dad, as your offspring I am glad.

THANK YOU, MY NURSE

As I lay there in hospital waiting upon deaths warm embrace.

I could see that sad look upon my nurse's face.

They saved me first with medicine and drips.

They filled me to the brim.

A few days later I go to greet them, with the warmest grin.

Oh, how you have saved my life in more ways than one.

For without you, my life would surely be gone.

You saw something in me.

You knew I'd be set free.,

I'll take over the reins from here I've got my full senses now.

This I know I can cope.

You are setting this man free with hope.

Take some credit now, for all your hard work.

For in the depths within my demons run, Watch with a bold big smirk.

You relit this man's sun.

You've saved me in more ways than one.

For without you my nurse I'd surely be gone.

WITHDRAWL

The darkness creeps upon me
As I face my sober reality

The bottle no longer a friend
But an enemy that I must defend

Withdrawal grips me like a vice
A darkness that feels like a sacrifice

My body shakes and trembles
As the withdrawal never dissembles

My mind races with fears and doubts
As the addiction urges me to pour it out

But I must fight this endless battle
And pray for strength to break this shackle

The darkness of alcohol withdrawal
Is a pain that never seems to stall

But I must push through the agony
And find the light of sobriety

I'll face the darkness and its pain
With the hope of sunshine and rain

For every step is a step towards healing
And every fight is a step towards revealing

The light that once was hidden deep
Buried beneath the bottles I would keep

Now I see the path that I must take
A life without alcohol, and the darkness it would make.

REHAB ARRIVAL

Walking up the drive with suitcase.

Making sure I'd tied my shoelaces.

Heart pounding, sweaty palms, my legs all so weak.

For here in this building inner peace, I seek.

I get to the door,

My eyes still focused on the floor.

No confidence, no me.

Just a plain man laid out for all to see.

It didn't take me long to settle in.

For this is the place I rid the demons from within.

The people are amazing, and strong,

For me to worry, I was wrong.

Laughter, tears and talking filled the quiet halls.

I could even say, I face this with balls.

I'd let my family know I was safe.

As my peers has welcomed me with a warm embrace.

These could be friends for a lifetime,

After all we'd been given the same lifeline.

Here my future stands before me,

Here I make myself *free*.

Holgate house, can you take me in?

Holgate house, can you stop me sin?

I found my higher power,

Not in some person or flower.

I found it in fate,

I believe that's what led me to your gate.

I was finally ready for rehab,

Just not the monthly kebab.

I'd let go of some people who I found didn't love me.

I give myself to this house to this home,

Now in the morning I don't wake up alone.

Goodbye to everything I leave in my past.

I'm so glad I ran and ran so fucking fast.

For here and to them I am worth something.

Welcomed with my serenity ring.

This house saved my life in more ways than one.

For without my peers and staff my life would surely be gone.

DEMONS RUN

They knew I was coming.

Coming for the things they say I'd never have.

The things of me that were lost in the pits of hell.

Now I just laugh as I watch my Demons run.

The scariest thing within my shadows are me.

This has released a man from anger and resentment.

He's back on form, he's no longer the devil inside me.

Now I just laugh as I watch my Demons run.

OUR NAMES

A recovery house full of twenty,

That's a few more than plenty.

I've never seen so much pain in one room,

In the darkest corners our demon's loom.

We're all here to heal and fight,

We were all give a second chance at light.

We share our darkest secrets of our past.

We pray for our sobriety, this time it must last.

We hug, we laugh, and we cry,

However, as a unit, we shine and try.

Crack head, smack rat, meth head, piss head

These are the names we are cruelly fed.

Clean and serene these are our names too

Don't judge too quick as these names can come for you.

That's when we welcome you with an open arm,

Then we make sure you come to no harm.

We will sit and listen, we'll cry too,

When we already know you've sneaked to top up in the loo.

No amount of deodorant or fresh mint.

Can rid you of your latest drinking stint.

3. A LETTER TO MY FOURTEEN-YEAR-OLD SELF

Dear Kieran,

      Today is the first time you're going to get drunk. Are you excited? Scared or nervous? Please don't, however I know it's too late to tell you this now.

I know today you had an argument with your dad. Don't worry, go easy on him. He's broken his own heart. His mind and conscience are not with it. I'm so sad to tell you. You're going to have to do the same one day as well. One day, but don't worry about that for now. However, dad is going to be there to pick up the little pieces of what left of you up.

So tonight, you're going to drink four cans of Foster's, you're going to hit on your sister's friends. Don't worry, you're going to wake up with no hangover, they won't start until next year.

I could shake you right now. I only beg of my higher power

how much I want to scream at you right now that alcohol is not the answer. I know you're afraid, I know how alone you are feeling.

Don't worry, you're about to get popular. All those nights spending awake, imagining your future, well guess what they're about to come true. I'm so excited about the journey you're about to embark on.

Kieran, over the next couple of years you're going to get lots of friends and go to lots of parties. You're going to spend a lot of time making lots of mistakes. Don't worry though. You're young you'll soon learn.

So, enjoy yourself, enjoy getting drunk at parties and sleeping around.

You're only young, you'll come through.

Your first proper job is coming as well. You'll feel like you're living the dream. If only I could tell you to save some of that money, you're going to need it one day.

Don't worry, you're young it's what you're supposed to do.

By now she has been gone for good, I'm sorry I let her hurt you, I didn't know she'd have done that to you.

Good news, you're about to fall in love for the first time. I'm sorry to say, you're going to break your own heart by leaving her, but you must. She's been cheating on you. You'll catch her; however, you'll get over this. Your worst heartbreak is yet to come, Unfortunately, I must promise you, you'll love again.

Don't worry though, you're young it's what you're supposed

to do.

You're nearly 20! You're about to get your first car, you're about to travel the world.

You're going to celebrate your 21st in Las Vegas! You're going travel across America at only twenty-one. I fondly look back on these memories, so please save them for me Kieran. Over the next couple of years, you'll travel the world. Don't worry, you can afford it. You're now working hard in Law. Enjoy it…. Whilst you can.

By now you have met the other three Important girls of your youth. You've removed them for your life, you knew they wasn't your soul mate. Don't worry a better stronger love is coming. Oh, if only you knew what I know now Kieran.

This is when life is going to throw you your biggest challenges. I'm sorry to tell you, you're about to get suspended from practicing law.

I know you got raped, and I know you can't deal with this. It will come back to you; it will haunt your dreams. Don't worry, I'll fix that for you.

Don't worry for now, still enjoy your life. You're young it's what you're supposed to do.

By now you'll be getting bored of daily drinking I imagine? You're about to buy your first Pub, at only twenty-seven. Congratulations on your downfall. Enjoy it whilst it lasts, the drinking and drugs too.

You've completed your goals, haven't you? Did that cause your arrogance. However, the reality is, you're waking up with the shakes and sweats, aren't you?

Still your biggest test is coming now, your biggest downfall, you're going to marry her, you'll regret that. If only I could tell you, what a controlling narcissist she really is. You wouldn't listen to everybody else tell you what she was really like, why would you listen to, me? You ignored everyone. If only you knew.

You're about to ring the police on your own Mother? Does that really sound like you?

Now you're asleep on a cot bed at your Dads. You're an alcoholic and a divorcee to be. Now you really have your rock bottom.

Well. Now we're catching up. Don't worry Kieran, I'm in Rehab, for you. I will fix our mistakes. I'll deal with the consequences. Cause I'm the adult now. It's what I'm supposed to do.

I'll catch up with you in a couple of months. Then together we'll restart our life.

Kieran – Aged 30.

4. QUOTES ON LOVE AND HEARTBREAK

HEARTBREAK

I stood by a woman, who only forsaken me.

She promised me, together forever. Until she didn't.

She wanted her sad lonely existence back. A door mat to somebody else. Anybody else.

She promised me happily ever after. After all what does that matter?

I fell out of love with her, then and there. I couldn't believe my ears.

The truth, the truth will set you free.

I could finally once and for all. Finally, be me.

She had stripped me of everything, mu looks pride and soul. I knew I'd have to go so I could once love me again and be gold.

I wish her the best in life, I'm just glad she's no longer my wife.

On to a bigger and better me. I can finally regenerate into somebody that's free.

CONGRATULATIONS

Congrats. You left him alone and broken. The one guy that ever truly cared about you. You abandoned him. The one person that never judged you even after you opened to him about everything.

The one guy that even in the end, treated you like his world.

But it's okay cause you're happy now. You may have shattered his idea and viewpoint of love, but it's ok. Really congrats, because there is no way he's caring about someone else the way he cared about you.

TRIGGER

Yes, you were the one pulling the trigger to hurt me but what's harder to admit is that it was me who handed you the bullets by letting you into my past trauma and pain. I didn't think you would use it as ammunition against me. We want to be known so badly we forget who may be loading the weapons as we speak to rob us of what we have left.

BOUNDARIES

Boundaries are necessary, they're not controlling a relationship. They're natural ways in which you protect yourself in a way. They are simply things you will and will not put up with in your life. Boundaries are healthy. Crossing boundaries is abuse.

HE WASN'T TOXIC

He was never the toxic person you believed him to be. He was funny, kind so caring to the point where he forgot to look after himself, He prioritised you and your happiness, and didn't care about anyone else. Yet you took him for granted and betrayed his trust. He didn't know where he went wrong and how to fix things. He began blaming himself and asking why he wasn't enough after everything he put into you. Now he's feeling unworthy of love because you treated him like an option while he treated you as his priority.

GOODBYE MY LOVE

There's a special place in hell for women like you.

The ones that lie when they look into your eyes and say I love you too.

Satan is waiting for you, with karma in his lap.

Cause all those lovely words you ever used was full of so much crap.

You didn't like the way I looked

Well, sorry you can get fucked.

I dress normal again.

My hairs not so much the same.

I'm not going to lie, you really did hurt me,

Let's be honest, you played the victim for anyone who'd see.

I hope one day you'll find someone who you love, like I loved you.

I hope someday they make you feel the same way I did too.

Then I hope it comes crashing down,

Then to get away, you leave town.

You think you destroyed me?

Well thanks to you, I'm free.

I hope you have enjoyed these words. I really hope you look.

Cause deep down I know you won't be in the second book.

Oh, darling Ex-Wife, I really did let you go,

After all the begging you did for some more cash flow.

You think I never saw your lies?

You think I never noticed your false alibis?

You used to call me names, a big girl,

I should act like a man.

Can you restart over?

Well, I know I can.

You really saw me as a pessimist

I just observed you as a narcissist.

You cared too much about a false reputation,

Well from your high paid waterboard job, you've finished your cleaner graduation.

Oh, darling Ex-Wife, you were my narcissist,

It was just a shame I was too blind and fell for it.

I'm just so glad I ran.

Whilst you live your boring life.

I'm doing everything I can.!

Smiling that you're not my wife.

5. A NARCISSISTS EXPOSURE

WHAT IS A NARCISSIST'S BIGGEST FEAR?

A narcissist's biggest fear is exposure.

Some narcissists will do anything to protect their reputation. They don't want anyone to know who they really are. They don't want people to know how abusive they are behind closed doors. Some people will go to any lengths to not let the public know what they are truly capable of. So please be careful who you expose, some toxic people can be extremely dangerous. Their fake reputation is their life.

Narcissists drive you to insanity with their criticisms, rudeness, accusations, cruelness, condemning, sense of superiority, riding their moral high horse, projection, hypocrisy, deaf ears, control, lies, threats, and double standards.

Then when you react, they say you are drama, and you are the one in need of help. They are the most immature blame shifters you will ever know, and full of nothing but excuses and justifications for their pathetic behaviours.

When addicts gets clean, we stay away from our dealer.
We don't call them to see if they are okay. We don't drive by their house, check their social media, or ask mutual friends for updates.
The narcissist in your life is your dealer.
Get clean.
No Contact.

ENDING A RELATIONSHIP WITH A NARCASSIST

Ending a relationship with a narcissist can be a challenging and difficult process, as they often struggle with accepting responsibility for their behaviour and may resort to manipulative tactics to maintain control. Here are some steps you can take to say goodbye to a narcissist:

1. Set boundaries: Before you say goodbye, it's important to establish clear boundaries with the narcissist to protect yourself from further emotional abuse or manipulation. Be firm and assertive about what you are willing to tolerate and what you are not.

2. Keep communication minimal: Limit your communication with the narcissist as much as possible. Keep conversations short and to the point and avoid getting drawn into arguments or emotional manipulation.

3. Seek support: Ending a relationship with a narcissist can be emotionally draining and stressful. Reach out to trusted friends, family members, or a therapist for support during this time.

4. Prepare for the narcissist's reaction: Narcissists often struggle with rejection and may react in unpredictable ways when you say goodbye. Be prepared for the possibility of emotional outbursts, attempts to guilt or manipulate you, or even threats.

5. Take care of yourself: Prioritise your own well-being and self-care during this process. Engage in activities that bring you joy and help you relax and focus on building healthy relationships with supportive people in your life.

Remember that saying goodbye to a narcissist can be a difficult but necessary step towards healing and moving forward in your life. Stay strong and stay committed to your own well-being.

5b. MY NARCASSIST'S EXPOSURE

Oh Dear,

You were my Narcissist, coming to terms with that was the hardest part of our marriage ending. The times I begged you to stop, when I'd done my research. That to make you feel more superior you had to belittle me, humiliate me, put me down, bully and abuse me. I got so involved with you, so quickly and so blindly.

The times I had to lock myself away and hide, in heartache. The pain you inflicted on me; How could you do that to someone you promised to love forever.

The truth was, I'd have done anything for you, I'd give you every penny I had. I'd have given you the world, In fact I did all that. And when it wasn't good enough for you. You still wanted more; it would never have been enough. You still accused me of cheating when all I wanted was family, friends and a life with you.

You had me trauma bonded and co-depended on you. I looked at you to make sure I was dressed the way you wanted me to, make sure I looked older than I was, less out there and plainer than any man would look. Make sure my beard was too long, or my hair was a mess. So, nobody would look twice at me.

All that was fine though, if it settled your insecurities. I did it. I cut off friends, so you didn't feel bad. I sacrificed my entire life to make yours better. Yet when it came to crunch time. You couldn't 't do the same for me.

You literally built us the perfect life to begin with, as narcissists do. The disguise you introduced me to was soon stripped back, Then I met you, you'd use affection as reward and punishment.

It got to the point even negative attention was attention that I all so craved to feel a slight glimmer of value.

I will say this though, I tried, more than any man should have tried. I fell for your narcotic charms; I thought I could live as a lesser human. Yet you kept pushing me towards my rock bottom.

One thing that always struck me as bizarre, you cut your life off. You cut your daughter off, no reason. You just ran away from your life to be with me. What was you running from? Now I know that was in the love bombing stage, when you acted like you loved me, that you were the happily ever after than only one man could dream of. Everything was perfect! Yet this was an illusion of a woman you just pretended to be.

I wrote in a quote, from your high paid waterboard job, congratulations on your cleaner graduation.

I didn't care what you did for a living or what company you worked for. So, what if you was a cleaner for a contractor company, You didn't have to pretend you was a big boss, at a waterboard. No wonder you couldn't change your name at work. They would have to see your lies on our marriage certificate. However, you worked! I really didn't care what you did. I know that Narcissists must feel superior to those who they hold in high esteem.

There is nothing wrong with you being a cleaner. You never had to lie.

Lying became a second language of our marriage. I eventually gave up on calling you out on your lies and deceit. I just thought and consciously thought, what's the point? You're going to lie, and if didn't really affect anything then why should I be bothered?

Do you know how hard it was to decide that? That the person who stood before their god, who promised to be honest to me to accept and allow them to tell lies?

Cause we all know, you can't ever expect two things from a Narcissist, honesty or an apology.

Everything was always my fault, you couldn't afford to live, and that was my fault. Although when we did join finances, I didn't get a say how you spent my money.

You judged me for my past? I never returned that favour and I'm thankful for never doing that. Did you know my closest friends are that scared of what you're capable of they couldn't warn me about you when we met? I've heard it all since, how you are a manipulator, a man eater, how you've used your Narcissist ways to split up marriages. and more importantly. Someone believes you're "Dangerous"

Dangerous! I never felt in danger, yet after therapy, I believe them.

There are so many parts of me, my essence that you brutally and cruelly stole from me. If you needed them, you're welcome to them. If they have been touched by you. I don't want them.

When I look back, I can't believe I allowed myself to be so controlled by another human being. I look back at living with you. How you used to hide me, sneak me in the house after a fall out. Only because you'd have made up the most horrendous lies about me, and you couldn't ever admit your dishonesty, that it resulted in me parking my car around the corner, coming in late at night. I allowed this too easily, you were my wife, and this was my home. Was I really that stupid?

To misquote Celine "I finished crying in the instant that I left"

You were done with me; I was done being your victim. What kind of person wants another person to be alone on Christmas Day. You wanted me in my car alone. All day, then when you found out I went to a friend's house. You got upset and again asked me to leave our home for the night again on Christmas Day. Cause I know now Narcissists must ruin every special occasion. We had to get married on my Birthday! Just so one day a year couldn't be just about me. It had to be about you too, whilst we were separated on my 30th Birthday, you came to me. I thought to win me back. It wasn't, it was to remove me from one of the few friends I had left. To only take me to my father's thinking I couldn't stay out and celebrate any longer.

I told you I had an issue with alcohol. That I wanted help. In the year I spent getting better, you were rarely if ever there at all.

You left my elderly father to pick up the pieces of me, the damage and destruction that you had caused. You'd pick me up, then do it all over again. How much joy did it bring you? You were supposed to love me? Why would you keep wanting me to fail?

I realised, you wanted me to fail, at every hurdle. So, you could play victim to my disease. You get to go to your support group and pretend how bad I was. Well, I'm sorry. I wasn't horrendous. I drank heavily and passed out. I couldn't apologise enough to you. You didn't care though. You never cared. You actually drank the same amount as I did. Just you was able to stop. You can't honestly say you didn't.

Everything was about perception with you. Nothing was honest. You had to look like you had money, or a business or something. Maybe that's why you go for men with pubs? Cause soon as you got mine, you barred every female that ever looked at me and burned every bridge we had.

When I think about the number you did on me, I'm heartlessly reminded of the tears I cried for you! For the times I wanted to hurt myself because you had conditioned me to believe I couldn't live without you in my life.

Well guess what you was right. Your biggest fear was realised. After rehab I wouldn't want you. Why would I want someone who abused me?

You literally took everything from me. I fell out of love with you, a line I once never thought I'd be able to say about you.

I honestly believed I was the bad person! I made excuses for your inexcusable behaviour. I'd apologise on your behalf.

The biggest turning point for me was when I saw your pure evil nasty side. Maybe you remember? You'd fallen asleep, you missed a parcel for somebody else. Cause you couldn't just be truthful. You then spoke to their customer services, the way you treated another human being was utterly disgusting, I'd never seen this side of you. It was evil.

I actually spend the next day phoning around making apologises for you.

Rehab taught me so much about Narcissism. What a damaging affect you had on me.

We spend our life wanting to be so known, that I literally gave you the bullets to fire at me and use against me, I gave you all the ammunition to hurt me. You actually enjoyed watching me in pain, especially when it wasn't yours.

After you lost our first pregnancy, I was there for you. Yeah, we changed the dynamic, convincing each other we wanted children. I don't know how many fake miscarriages followed this. Knowing I wanted a child more than anything. You'd lie to me, saying you were pregnant then fake a miscarriage. Funny how they only ever happened when I wasn't around.

I remember all the lies you told about going to the hospital. All the lies you told to fake illnesses, strokes, cancer, pregnancies. I let you live in your fantasy world.

I even sat your daughter down, to tell her you wasn't well, That you'd been in hospital after a stroke. The Stroke you probably never had.

I think another final straw had to be how you asked me to pass a message to your late Grandma through my dying Grandma, cause of course I couldn't grieve, it had to be about you.

Your behaviour towards me during our marriage was abusive, and it has taken me a very long time to come to terms with how it affected me.
Your constant criticism, your need for control and your manipulative behaviour left me feeling worthless and powerless.

I turned to alcohol as a way to cope with the pain and the stress. It became my escape, my way to numb the feelings of anxiety and depression that were a constant presence in my life.

But the more I drank, the worse things became. My addiction only fuelled your anger and your aggression towards me. I felt trapped, like I was drowning and there was no way out.

It wasn't until I hit rock bottom that I realised something had to change. I knew that I couldn't continue living my life this way. I made the decision to leave, to get help and to finally take control of my life.

It hasn't been easy, but I am slowly starting to heal. I am learning to love myself again, to find happiness in the simple things and to appreciate the beauty of life. It has taken a lot of work, but I am finally starting to feel like I am on the path to recovery.

It always had to be about you. Everything. Not anymore. It's about me now.

So now I'm building a new life. One that doesn't involve you. Will never do again. This is my closure to you Ex-Wife. You are my narcissist, and this is your exposure. I think I'll forever be grateful that you could never complete the cycle and discard me first.

Cause as you said, you've broken up with everyone you've ever been with. Not this time. This time I learned of the sick games you play, and I ran!

I ran so fast. As soon as I knew I was done. I got my spot with the rehab I wanted. The truth is, they knew I was co-depended to you and in a trauma bond, they was actually waiting for us to be over before they'd allow me in. They knew I needed to be away from you in order to recover.

Unfortunately, you may see your exposure as a resentment on my behalf. I can assure you it's not. I fully believe in Karama, that one day you will answer to what you did to me.

However, this book is to help those people affected by several issues, one being having a narcissist spouse. Well, if I could break free from you. Knowing how attached I was to you. Well, anyone reading this be rest assured they can do it to.

All I can say is life is better without a narcissist, a drama triangle and the pure and utter chaos that you get dragged in.

The only thing I don't think I will ever understand, how you can have no remorse for being so cruel to a person, especially someone who loved you as much as I did.

The moment I realised that I was being manipulated and controlled by my narcissistic ex-wife was a difficult and painful one. Since the beginning , I had been in a relationship that I thought was loving and supportive, but as time went on, I began to realise that something was not quite right.

It started with little things, like you constantly criticising me and making me feel like I was never good enough. You would belittle my accomplishments and make me feel small and insignificant.

Over time, your behaviour became more and more controlling, and I found myself walking on eggshells around you, afraid of setting off your anger.
It wasn't until I started doing research on narcissism that I began to see the truth about my situation. I realised that I was

in a relationship with a narcissistic abuser, and that you had been manipulating and controlling me the whole time.

I also realised that I was co-dependent on you and that I was in a trauma bond, which made it difficult for me to leave the relationship. Even though I'd keep trying you'd always promise you would change, things would be different, and then you'd just pull me back.
 I had become so accustomed to your behaviour that I didn't even realise how much damage it was doing to me.

The moment of realisation was painful and overwhelming, but it was also a turning point. I knew that I had to take action and break free from the toxic cycle that I had been caught in for so long.

It wasn't easy, and it took a lot of work to break free from the trauma bond and start rebuilding my life. But looking back, I know that it was the right decision. I am now in a healthy and loving relationship, and I have taken steps to heal from the emotional scars of my past.

I hope that you can understand the impact that your behaviour had on me. I don't hate you, but I can no longer be a part of your life. I found my own sense of peace. I hope that you can do the same.

I'll end with this,

God, Grant me the serenity to accept the things I cannot change, the courage to change the things I can and the wisdom to know the difference. I had courage to change us. To leave, you wanted me to accept the way you cruelly treated me. You actually said those words 'accept the things you cannot change". No thank you, I had the courage to leave, I was granted the wisdom to know the difference,

6. QUOTES ON HEALING FROM HEARTBREAK

M6

My drives down the M6 don't feel quite the same,

Cause I can't say Hey Siri and tell it to call your name.

But I've learnt that's not a bad thing cause I've got more time to sing.

The thought of that would once destroy me but now it only brings me peace and I don't even think to ring.

My drives down the M6 don't feel quite the same cause if I said Hey Siri, it wouldn't even recognise your name.

I GAVE UP ON YOU

Okay yeah, I gave up on you, but you need to understand how much that took out of me

I gave you endless chances. I always had your back and I truly accepted you for who you were.

When the rest of your life didn't want you. I did...

Okay yeah, I gave up on you, but you need to understand that took everything that was inside me to leave you alone

All the sleepless nights. All the miscommunication

I gave you everything that I had to give, and I made you my world and it still wasn't enough

So, I had to choose me. Finally, I chose me.

DO I HATE YOU?

Hate you? No, I don't hate you, but I'm no longer the hopeless romantic you once knew.

So, no I don't hate you. But I do hate, there's a hole in my sleeve from where my heart used to be. That there's doubt in my mind when someone tells me they love me.

I now roll my eyes at romantic movies I once loved. There was a time I thought that would be us one day, but I guess I misjudged.

I can no longer get excited when my heart begins to race. I'll self-sabotage, run away, just in case because as we know infatuation and immense highs will only end in catastrophic lows and terminal goodbyes.

Love no longer feels innocent, sweet or something to be desired or deserved. It feels wrong, deceitful, nothing to be admired.

I no longer to allow myself to picture happy endings. What's the point? When. It will only lead to a heart immune from mending.

I hate that P! NK, M&M's and Flamingos will never be the same.

Haunted memories that will forever echo your name.

So, no I don't hate you.

But I do hate I will never be able to love like I used to.

MY OTHER ADDICTION

I got addicted to you so easily.

Attracted to you in ways I can't explain. I only wanted your attention to be honest.

I cared about you more than you think. I thought about you more than you realise. I appreciated you more than you will ever know.

No words were amazing enough to describe how fantastic you once made me feel.

You was the first and the last thing on my mind each and every day.

That being said. I got addicted to me instead.

Attracted to myself in ways I can't explain. I only want my attention to be honest.

I care about me more now than I ever thought I'd think. I think about me more than I ever have. I appreciate me more than I will ever know.

No words are amazing enough to describe how fantastic I now make me feel.

I am the first and the last thing on my mind each and every day.

FOND MEMORIES

One day you will look back on me fondly and realise I loved you with all I was, unconditional love, no one would have loved you the way I would have, yet you decided you didn't want it, but when you look back years from now, that regret will hit hard because I loved you with all I am, and I would have walked through hell for you and loved you for an eternity.

I said what I said.

I MISSED YOU

Yeah, there was a time I missed you, yeah, I missed how it used to be, I even told you that. Yet life's too short to dwell on what happened. Each single minute is another chance to be happy. So, I'm going to live my life every minute of every day. And hey, I don't want you in it. There's no room for you. I moved on.

UNTITLED

I used to think that you didn't love me. Your need to control my every action and then blame me for being terrible and a disappointment when I didn't fit into your mould screwed up my perception of myself, which in turn made me think I wasn't worthy of good things. Then one day, it just sort of hit me... it's not that you didn't love ME, you weren't capable of loving anyone for who they are, yourself included.

And justified it with your closed-minded way of seeing those around you.

Perception is a dangerously ugly thing at times when those you are trying to prove your worth to are convinced, they have to be perfect and everyone else is beneath them. Stay away from those that try to validate their self-induced blindness with the inability to recognise the humanness of those around them, including their own imperfections.

SENTENCING

If they get you to the point where you consider destroying yourself to prove your love,

You run.

You run! And you don't ever look back.

Imagine another year of not being considered, of not being heard, of not being seen. Imagine five more, ten more, twenty more spirit shattering, soul crushing years.

That goodbye was a blessing.

NOT THIS TIME

No.

Not this time.

You are not allowed back.

No, not this time.

Because this time, I choose me.

Me over this.

Me over you.

I LOST THE MOST IMPORTANT PERSON. ME.

I never thought the words I don't love you anymore would every come out of my mouth. I'd have done anything for you. I sacrificed myself to make you happy. I lost myself in you finding yourself. Supporting you. I gave you the bullets to cause me pain so you could revel and live in.

SOMETIMES

Sometimes you have to go through it. you have to feel it. Cry over it. Hurt. Burn and even die a little, you know? Pain is one of those things we have to accept. One of those things that come to us when we least expect it. You know we all wish we didn't have to, but it is inevitable. To feel it in our souls. To feel it when someone else is going through it. This is our truth. This is what connect us. How we relate to each other... no matter what language we speak or where we come from. I understand you. I understand what you're going through... and I want to tell you that you are not alone. That you will overcome all of it sooner or later. That you were built for it. To walk through the fire. To heal from it. To come back even stronger than before. Because this is what we have to go through to grow. To move on. To share. To experience one another. To gain the wisdom of life and love. Pain is a part of our lives. Some of us tend to feel it more deeply than others. But you are not alone. I feel it too. Right now, in this very moment. I feel it too! and I just want to let you know... how everything will turn out. How everything soon will make sense and how everything you deserve will come back to you... the way it was supposed to come back to you. every broken part of you will find its way. Every missing part will soon find their way back home.

LEARNING TO UNLOVE

I did not unlove you overnight.

No, I unloved you in bits of pieces over time.

I grew a new skin that you could never touch, a new heart that you could never break, and a new soul that you could never corrupt.

This is how I unloved you...

Slowly, painfully,

But with no regrets.

PRIDE

I'm proud of the person

I'm becoming.

My mindset has changed

My priorities have changed.

My taste has changed.

My tolerance has changed. I'm evolving.

FORGIVNESS

You took the best of me. I forgive you

You caused the worst in me. I forgive you.

You stole me. I forgive you.

You lied, was disloyal, you betrayed me. I forgive you.

You took advantage of me. I forgive you.

You broke my heart. I forgive you.

You stole the sun from my day. I forgive you.

You made me think love wasn't ever going to happen for me again. I forgive you.

You taught me not to wear my heart on my sleeve. I forgive you.

You destroyed me, inside and out. I forgive you.

I let you into myself, gave you the parts of me you needed so freely.

I let you become more important in my life than me.

I let you bully me, hurt me, made me cry. Make me feel so worthless that I didn't want to be alive.

I let you in. I forgive me.

I forgive me.

7. FOUR WEEKS BEFORE REHABILITATION

Four weeks before my final detox, I call this cold turkey detox, as Christmas Day 2022 was the final time I would ever relapse. An believe me, the circumstances which lead me to my relapse was cold.
At the end of our marriage my ex-wife had been attending Wednesday night support meetings, these meetings were intended to support the families of people suffering with addiction,
My ex-wife used these to play the victim of my disease. She loved the compassion and social aspect more than the fundamental purpose of what my sponsor had arranged for her.

That being said, during the times she did attend, she got friendly with one of the facilitators. Later it would transpire that this facilitator was also a councillor at a Rehabilitation Facility. I remember receiving the call. My ex-wife had rung me to tell me the good news! I'd been trying to get into a Rehabilitation facility since July, The news was I'd been given a place at this Rehab!

Since I got that news, I'd tried anything to get a proper detox. It's unfortunate to say, unless you pay out your nose, or you have other medical illnesses you really don't have too many options, I tried everything, but couldn't get a detox. However, this was my shot?! I had no choice, everything was going to rest on this, I needed five days sober time before admittance to the facility.
The only way to do this was Cold Turkey!
I was off, determined not to let myself down. I did it though, on my own.

If you've ever withdrawn from Alcohol, I can tell you Delirium Tremors are not pretty to watch, let alone to experience. However, over the next seven days I would detox myself. One minute at a time.
I'd done it! I was sober. Proud I'd done it alone. Surely you must see how much going in here meant to me.

The downside from this, I would be away for Christmas time, the one day of the year for family. Selfishly in order to what I thought was to save my marriage, I didn't care. I need this.

I would however later to go on and have a conversation with my ex-wife, we agreed it was for the best. I did hesitate, why was she far too eager to agree to lose me?
Monday comes, my assessment. The assessment to my future, the assessment to what is about to come.

There I was, standing at the gates of A NEW, my future in front of me right here.

If it sounds too good to be true, it probably is.
As soon as I entered the building, I felt uncomfortable and totally unrelaxed.
They led my ex-wife and I into the lounge area.
My ex-wife's first comment, one of which should have thrown massive red warning flags; however, I was so numb to the control. "Oh, look there's a camera above the TV. I can ask the facilitator how you're getting on!"
I never said a word.
Then in comes Mark, I thought he was waiting for his audition for SAS: Who dares wins.

Mark is the Rehab manager. He also had another woman with him.
Mark told us both a lot about the rehab, the programme, how the process worked. Emphasising the strict regime. Apparently, if he asked me to jump, he wanted a reply with how high? Without hesitant or question. Even if it was unjustified or extreme.
Mark then turned the conversation to how the programme and more importantly him would "Strip the addict from within me." Then he would show me how to rebuild myself. That I was evil and have done evil things.

Yet he was positive he knew there was a good guy underneath. Although even by this time, I was too uncomfortable to speak. His attention soon got drawn to my ex-wife. Who sat there smiling, thinking he was in her words. "Getting the better of me." Whilst the addict in me was actually sitting there already think, how easy it would be to manipulate this man, he was unaccredited and thought he knew best. I knew then, I needed a proper rehabilitation where they could see these behaviours I have picked up and help me deal with them and change. Not punish me.

So, Mark asks, my ex-wife about my drinking, who rarely saw my drinking and have little insight, she was always too busy to cope with the drama.
Surely, he should be asking me. After all. I'm the one with the Disease.
Mark straight out arrogantly asked me if I'd honoured my vows. I didn't say anything other than "No." If I'd had said yes, I'd been, and liar and my falsely disguised perfect wife sat next to me would have agreed.

Inside I was saddened. I actually thought Mark, you don't know anything about how much of a sham my marriage has become, how the woman I met was a false disguise to leer me into her Narcissistic Charms. Then remove the disguise and I'd forever be under her spell. Abused, worthless and nothing.

My diagnosis for drinking, had already been given to me, I've been fundamentally unhappy for a very long time.
I just remained calm, sat content on the couch. I couldn't show any emotion or how his absurd question did affect me, I knew if I didn't get into this rehab, my marriage would surely be over. The woman introduced herself, she said she had been through the process herself. She said it was hard work however, the best boot camp I would ever do.

Then came the rules.
No contact with the outside world for the first month at all.
Then it was weekly phone calls only.
No Phone for three months. Or at least until you move onto second stage for another three months.
It's then I saw my ex-wife's face light up the room. I couldn't speak to my friends or family. Just her, once a week.

It was then I was looking at admittance within the new year.
I instantly saw the resentment within my ex-wife's face.

I know things were bad at home, how could you want your husband to be in a place worse than prison? A hell hole?
I realise now looking back, how much respect I lost for her in that moment, to feed her own egotistical ideology and to carry on playing like the world was against her, she'd put me through this?
A NEW wanted me to go to a Pre-Hab, session that afternoon. I attended. I could only describe the leaders as brainwashed into believing they were horrible people. They'd put one of them on a clothing ban just two days into their treatment, I was horrified.

I spoke to my alcohol care Nurse, Who immediately had their reservations. They said they feared this place was going to cause trauma and be physiologically damaging.
I later told my ex-wife about this; she dismissed it as one person's opinion.

The topic of Christmas had come up. Turned out one of her children didn't want me there Christmas Day. Now, Finally I understood. She wanted rid of me, because she never stood up for me before hand, why would she now?
Instantly and in defensive mode, she tried to tell me she thinks I don't want to go to A NEW because I was scared. Damn right I was! But not because I was intimidated. I saw the bigger picture.
Now she definitely would have the tools to play victim to my disease.

Fast forward to Christmas day, We'd already previously discussed I'd spend the day in my car and come back in the evening. As not to make me be in my home, with my ex-wife on Christmas day an issue. I was surprisingly alright with this.
I woke up in the morning and went downstairs. I said I'll have a brew and go.
She asked me if I minded if I didn't, as her daughter would soon

be there,
I obliged and left.

Whilst in my car, I saw a friends status update about Taxi fares. I offered her a lift. Whilst I was driving, she offered me to stay for Christmas Dinner. You know what I did.
My ex-wife later texts me to tell me her guests had left. I returned home, she'd enquired to what I've been up to all day. I told her exactly what I'd done. Immediately she was more than pissed off. Cause apparently, she was under the impression I'd randomly turn up and apologise to her family and friends. For reasons unknown.
The reality was, she was unhappy I didn't spend Christmas Day alone in my car as my punishment for my previously relapse. We'd already had a conversation day early, how she wanted me to spend Christmas alone, to see how she would be feeling.

Punishment and rewards. That's how our marriage had ended up.

She then asked me to leave. I rightly asked why, and all hell broke loose.
The argument ended I was nothing and worthless to her, I'd stopped financing her life and she was ready to discard me. I was and am worthless to her., I couldn't spend just one day reflecting on my behaviour and not going to ANEW. I snapped finally and said, So I'm under lock and key, and you get perfect tabs on me, whilst you do what you want. In my head I'm thinking you've had your single male friends round whilst I've been at my Lesbian and her partner's house. Who actually wanted me on Christmas Day.

I told her, there and then about my feelings towards ANEW, she would hold it over me as she'd organised it and it entitles her to play the victim in our marriage.
Finally, I seen the Narcissist in front of me. She didn't love me,

or she never loved me. I got my coat and left.

I knew then, I would never return to her, or her warped mind. I was free from her trap.

However, knowing deep down. It was the end; I wasn't going to ANEW.
I had nothing. FUCK IT BUTTON PRESSED!

I went to my fathers with a bottle of Whiskey, the drinking ensued. Waking up, drinking, being sick. Pissing the bed, crying only to fall asleep and do it all over again.
I got a few texts from my ex-wife, wanting me back, as it was close to pay day. To this day, I've never responded.
She loved telling me she went to my home AA meeting, as someone from her group wanted to go. She just concreted to me, that even after we'd separated, she still wanted to play the innocent victim.

Anybody knows, you shouldn't leave an alcoholic alone at Christmas.
The drinking continued until one morning I awoke vomiting massive amounts of blood. I'd further go on all day doing this. Till I couldn't even keep alcohol down. This is when the withdrawals started. Then the seizures. My poor father had enough, he phoned for an ambulance. Upon arriving at hospital, I was rushed into resus.

The movement had gone from my body, I couldn't function.
My alcohol care nurse had convinced a consultant to medically detox me. Thank the lord!
He then ensured I go an emergency placement at a Rehab Facility. A real one. Based on strengths and power.
All of which had been stripped from me.
Once I was discharged it was confirmed. I was going to Holgate House, Lancashire.

I attended regular appointments preparing me for a proper rehab, not a prison sentence.
Somebody had seen my worth, even if I couldn't see it myself.
Just remembering how low I felt in my life. How shrunken I was and Invisible.
How I felt like I didn't matter. My thoughts didn't matter. My emotions, needs and feelings ignored.

Somebody had seen how fundamentally unhappy I was, completely drained and exhausted.
Therefore, now this is why I choose to be me. I refuse to shrink myself to fit somebodies' else idea of what a worthwhile human is. For once I've chose myself.

8. WHAT MY ADDICTION LED ME TO

Powerless over alcohol.

Powerless to me means you lose all self-control, will power, defence strategies and walls. You feel completely vulnerable.

You literally have no choice in anything. You can't persuade, inform, choose or negotiate. You have no choice in anything. You can't surrender as you have no option at all.

Nothing you can do will change the inevitable outcome.

You can with the best will in the world try. Any attempts of regaining any sense of responsibility, power, choice or even pure will; they will all be met with complete failure.

Powerless means you are at the mercy of your own addiction.

Hence the term Addiction.

When I have personally been powerless, I have never felt more vulnerable.

I admitted I was 100% powerless over alcohol. It was a kind friend when I was delusional enough to believe this. It rapidly became my worst enemy.

I know prior to my first detox and after I admitted I was Alcohol Dependant, any trigger, emotion or even happy feelings were all just excuses to drink.

I created an entire career and lifestyle to suit my drinking.

The only way I can describe it now, looking back is Alcohol cruelly chose me. It took over me quickly. Without my knowledge.

Any sober periods were eventually met with relapses prior to working my programme.

After my first major detox it was harder to relapse, but it could happen.

Drugs have been a part of my life at fifth teen years old. When I was groomed. Mainly taking ecstasy in school and missing 5th period. Sitting in the toilets. Pardon the phrase but completely off my noodle. Ecstasy stayed consistently in my life until I was around 18 years old, until it phased of as a part of my former years.

I went down a dark path in my later twenties when cocaine would be an issue.

Although during the end of my drinking I am confident I

would have taken any mind-altering substance to remove the pain, depression, heartache and despair I was feeling. I allowed myself to get that blackout drunk to try and feel numb, to try to sleep. To try and not feel anymore. In hindsight I was trying to supress my own humanity,

Therefor I am complete powerless over any mind-altering substance. That's why I call myself an Addict.

When I was fifteen years old, I met an older woman. One who I idolised and wanted to impress. She was early 40's, single mother. Who described herself as loving toy boys. The irony of that phrase now, all I was, a toy to her. This woman introduced me to drugs and Lambrini,

I would often go to her house and stay over. I lied to my parents and invented a whole new person so they would never find out. Even then the lies were there to aid my drinking and using. Although this situationshop would quickly develop. She would utterly fuel me with substances. Although at first, we did do physical things, we never actually had sex until she had waited until I was sixteen, Oh the morals of an addict. I was sixteen before she made her final move on me. Here, then. NOW, the dangers appeared. However, I was young and naive, in redefection you could have spilled the future out for me, and I'd have probably gone along with it anyway to impress somebody.

She told me she had fantasies, at sixteen if a woman whose experienced mentions a fantasy, it's like ecstasy to your stupid dumb ears.

She wanted to watch me fuck somebody else. Apparently, it would be fun, and I would enjoy it. I'd like to say, I realised it was weird and I got out. That's a fairy tale. This is a book on how I survived addiction. The abuse went on for the next year or. So many different people. It got to the point she wasn't even in the room anymore. Apparently, she was "Getting Off" Imaging what I was doing, more than actually watching or participating.

The final time this happened, I'd have finished with who I was upstairs with, and they lay on me and said, "You're well worth your money you." I cry at the ink of the page, not only had I been used and abused, but it was also for monetary gain for somebody else. Who had the right to sell my body! It's mine! I felt dirty and used. I'd been groomed and abused. I was too young, I'd really lost my innocence, I'd gotten tangled up in some adventure.

Looking back, I feel guidable and naive. I thought I was intelligent. I remember thinking how cool I thought I was, the best. Only now do I realise on how many dangerous situations I was in at the time due to a false sense of arrogance. I would never have done any of that if I wasn't using. I was a danger to myself, my sexual health. I was too young; I feel like now I have lost years because of that woman. Even some of my old feelings of low self-worth always stemmed from this. For years afterwards I believed that's what I was only good for.

In my late teenage years, I got into huge amounts of debt. With Credit Cards and Loans etc… Most of this actually went on Alcohol or holidays, nothing serious like an education. It took me and my parents a lot to pay back nearly £30,000 worth of debt back.

Looking back, I don't think the years of stress following this was worth it at all. I remember not sleeping because of stress, then drinking to sleep.

I once turned up at work drunk, nobody knew, however my performance was less than minimal. I let the team down that day. I felt at the time, it's only McDonald's what do I care? Looking back, I can't believe how irresponsible this was. Totally unsafe too.

I once stormed out after an argument with my parents, I stormed out into the pub. Spending the day and night telling people how my parents just didn't understand me. How they caused unnecessary stress. How? I don't remember what the argument was even over. However, I remember blaming them for my drinking that day. All I was doing was complaining to other alcoholics finding yet more reasons in our pitiful existence to carry on drinking. I betrayed my parents, cause no matter what the argument was over, they'll have just wanted to help me. I feel pretty shitty looking back at this. I wish I could remember what it was over so I could apologise, I do remember retuning home pissed and passing out on the bathroom floor. We laugh now, but my stepfather still shows me pictures.

During my education years, Id' frequently use drug and alcohol together. Desperately trying to have the best night yet. Determined to have memories made. Even though most of the time, I'd awake and have forgotten the night before.

I ignored all the warnings, from tutors, teachers, support workers. It's like my education or at least the subjects never happened.

This were strange, the times, the behaviours I'd exhibited. Taking drugs off strangers, Getting so drunk without caring how I'd get home. If I had no money. I'd just pick a full drink up off the smokers table, when they couldn't take glasses outside.

I was in so much danger, but never really knew it. Or was conscious enough to realise the poor decision-making process in my alcoholic brain was making,

When I was around twenty-three years old, I had the naked incident. I want to laugh, yet the danger of this wants me to cry. I'd been on a night out with some friends. Drinking in a bar. I'd been drinking heavily that night. I'd got separated from my friends.

I found a bar later on and continued the festivities alone. That's the last thing I remember. Then it's all; a black out. I awoke early in the morning naked on a flat block stair. My hoody and shoes missing. My jeans next to me on the floor. Still to this day I don't know what happened or even how I managed to get there. I remember feeling very vulnerable, scared, shame and guilt. Just writing this I realise how dangerous this was. As to this today I still don't know what happened or how on earth I managed to end up there that evening.

In my very early days of daily drinking my Mum had an accident which meant she couldn't work. She was off work at the Pub she cleaned at. When I learnt this, I was straight in with the offer to help. I easily volunteered. It meant I could drink at 11am, why wouldn't I? I mean I'd worked all morning. That was my excuse.

I would get there at 9am, be let in, clean the Pub. Finishing by sitting at the bar between 11am – 3pm. I'd go to another Pub to hide just how much I drank daily. I'd be home by 11pm to repeat this vicious daily cycle.

Looking back, I could have drove to work., So I wouldn't be able to drink. Yet why would I? I wouldn't get that so hard worked for pint in the morning,

I'd sit in the company with other Alcoholics at 11am. All of us looking for excuses to drink in the morning.

Even though we all did this every day, following the same pattern. I could easily drink 10 – 15 pints every day and still maintain that I was apparently sober. Only I ever truly knew that my drinking was getting out of control.

I remember attended my friend's wedding, conniving myself it was weird that nobody was dancing with their tie on their head. This was completely illogical. I am being the idiot I am, and of course only drunk Kieran could rectify this. So true to my nature I got up. I requested karaoke. Put my tie on my head and went for it.

I'm face palming my sheet of paper and my inexcusable behaviour.

I thought I was being funny and entertaining. I was the life and soul. When upon pure sober thinking I was a dick! I made a total fool of myself. I wasn't funny, and I just acted like and dick. Looking back with my friends we do laugh at this at one of them stories. However, inside I know I was out of line,

A doctor once told me he thought I was withdrawing from Alcohol. I told him I wasn't. How or why, I don't know. I didn't even know what withdrawals were at the time. I of course denied it. I remember telling the Doctor off and impolitely reminding him he was a locum. Only to later report him to patient services, for outing my drinking.

I attended a meeting with the Practice Manager a week later. Sober and not withdrawing. She removed my visit from my record and said that the Dr wouldn't be back at my surgery again. Looking back if this was withdrawal, I feel massive guilt. This poor Doctor just wanted to help me, and I verbally degraded him and manipulated the situation for my own personal gain. I hope to this day his reputation wasn't damaged by this.

At the start of the decline in the ability to stop drinking alcohol, when I still had some control. I'd discreetly taper my alcohol use. So, I could have sober periods to avoid suspicion.

I remember a regular customer of a pub telling me their doctor had told the two have alcohol free weeks.

As I was still in denial this is what I decided to do, taper and have periods off the booze. I'd taper over 3-4 days, only drinking enough to hide the withdrawals, cutting my alcohol down and would spend several weeks sober. However just a dry drunk.

Only now as an acceptation alcoholic do I realise that I was tapering at the time. I'd just say I'm being good.

I used to actually say it was my job to drink, I used to say that in the pub trade it was expected for me to drinking, I mean I had to be the host with the most. Upon reflection, I orcrastrated my whole lifestyle to support my drinking.

I remember thinking I was at the top of my game., That my hard work had paid off.

Oh, how wrong I was. I'd soon be Alcohol Dependant; little did I know what I was letting myself in for. I wish I never missed these warnings.

Whilst I had my own pub, after I'd crossed that all so talked about line. I was hiding spirits upstairs, only to drink to stop the shakes throughout the day. Stupidly believing that could control my drinking.

After a year or so, I had my own group of friends and then the partying started. I'd let my friends stay till the early hours, justifying it by not charging them for Alcohol so I didn't lose my liquor license. I was having sex with whoever I wanted to, seeing some of these people as trophies and just using them for my own sexual gratification.

During this time, I was drinking heavily and stimulating myself in only ways I know how.

There was one girl, who I massively mistreated, I used her. I didn't show her the respect she deserved, she truly cared about me. Yet I was too involved with substances to realise I was doing this. We'd laugh late at nights, about how drunk we were, like it was party time at the palace and how fun we was. The reality is we were just as a pair of drunks.

I sit here, clean I wouldn't ever imagine myself disrespecting someone in this way at all.

This is a time of my life where I thought I genuinely had it all. I had everything I was wanted. In hindsight I hated every minute of it. I never want to own a pub again.

I never want to drink again.

Over this time, I contracted and STI. I'd not open the pub out of laziness. On the days I did I get up, I'd drink immediately to make me feel better, so I could function.

More spirits to balance myself out.

I remember even doing things I really shouldn't have done. In front of people like it was a game. It was pure repulsive behaviour. My mother would have been so disappointed in me.

All because I was stupid, immature and fancied making a show of myself.

I loss so much income, staff loss income. I encouraged my staff to drink to more than excess.

During the pub I actually used people and when they didn't fit in with the ever-evolving lifestyle I'd ghost their friendship. Writing this I feel the guilt in the pits of my being. How other people must have felt, all for what, my using?

How I really hurt people, that really cared for me.

I used to set my alarm for 10:30am, knowing I could put some booze in my system before the staff arrived so I could hide the withdrawal symptoms, this progressed so I couldn't hide it. So, I'd go to other local pubs and drink there. Again, only myself knowing just how much I was actually drinking, I'd constantly make plans around and surrounding booze, I'd never put myself in an alcohol-free situation.

I'd actually pay for other people's drinks so I wouldn't have to drink alone. I'd purposely manipulate people so I could just appear the life and soul of the party and carry-on drinking without a guilty conscience with very little consequences. I'd know people would feel compelled to drink with me being a pub landlord. I knew people would want to impress me, so I would use this to my advantage. If they wanted a party. I'd have organised this in my head and which bars and clubs we would be going to.

At the time I felt popular and accepted. Only on reflection do I look back and just feel used, because I owned a pub of all the people, I partied with none ever kept in touch afterwards.

I remember once a member of my staff made reference to how much I drank, I remember being really angry by this as then I really believed myself, I didn't have a drinking problem. However, with how much they drank who were they to judge? They was the problem, merely just projecting on to me.

It was the night before my wedding., I closed the pub early so we could get everything organised. I'd already part fallen out with my mum, thanks to the poison that was being fed to me by my ex-wife, However my family turned up at the pub that night. To try and save me, to try and stop the wedding, They'd found out about my narcissist. The narcissist I was marrying. They had the truth about her. No wonder she'd do anything to alienate me from me in the months that followed. My sister begged to get to me, to save me, even making the mistake of threating to break something to get my attention.

I wouldn't listen, I was already under the control of my narcissist then. I wasn't letting anyone ruin our special day. (I laugh at myself on the realisation of writing this)

So, the alienation started now, my ex-wife knew she had been sussed, so she would strategically alienate me from all my friends and family.

My ex-wife threatened me with leaving if I didn't ring the police to put a restraining order on my own Mother. Even getting herself witnesses so she could feel superior,

This was my Mum. Reflecting all I can think is what have I do. What possessed me to ever agree to this?

The police told my family no contact with me from now on.

I got pissed that night, I wish to anyone or anything, if I could go back and do that night over the other party would have been discharged from my life that night,

However, my narcissist had won, me all to herself.

When the proverbial line was crossed, into serious Alcohol Dependency. My health suffered massively. I'd wake up in the morning frequently retching and bringing up pure bial. I'd have constant diarrheal, sorry but morning withdrawals are not pretty and I'm not leaving out the details. This addiction is real. I'd be bloated from the gas from the twenty pints the day before. I gained humongous amount of weight; I remember my situation being horrendous. Yet stupidly continued to drink daily. Ignoring the decline to my health. Looking back, I was stuck with no way out, even then. I feel disappointed in myself for not reaching out any sooner, maybe just maybe if I'd have gotten help?

When I got married, I did calm down, I heavily reduced my alcohol intake. Yet it soon crept back in, my ex-wife being a heavy drinker also didn't help.

We moved pubs, to run one together. This was a huge mistake. I stupidly managed to convince myself that this was a fresh start. I had no choice, I had to control my drinking.

The first couple of weeks were great. We didn't drink till gone 5pm and then I only drank Pints of Mild. Nothing too heavy. I was always up early; the accounts were done.

It didn't last long, As Christmas approached Spirits, Shots and Bombs were back.

Then came the day drinking before long the hiding of the alcohol was back, I was drinking like the old days, which had started to seriously affect my health, even causing a mini stroke.

I remember feeling like a failure. Faking illnesses to stay in bed and have my ex-wife run the pub alone.

One of the only times I actually let her down.

I look back now and utterly hate ever signing for that pub it caused friction in my marriage due to finances. Caused friction between us and customers. It was a rough pub. I was an in-denial Alcoholic. My ex-wife was constantly controlling as she believed the pub to be hers, she wanted out as it was too much like hard work. We left to go home.

I put some money aside, once moving out of the pub. We could take some well-deserved time off. Go on that honeymoon, I'd set aside about £10,000 to last us. We spent it on Alcohol, bills and takeaways.

When we moved into the house, even though we were both drinking daily already, and heavily. I would organise leaving the house around restaurants or pubs that served food.

Never actually wanting to eat but doing so knowing we could stay all day and carry-on drinking., We'd come home and carry-on drinking until one or both of us passed out. This again was a daily repetitive process. Writing this I just remember how low myself esteem during this time actually was, I would never make an excuse to drink. I think at the time I used alcohol to escape a sad existence and a fundamentally unhappy life.

As I had the pub, I'd sort of got a full DJ set up by the end of it. When we moved into the house, I'd started to accept DJ Gigs, not because we need the money, but it was an easy excuse to drink. I'd explain to the wife. DJs have to drink otherwise I'd look miserable and wouldn't be able to play to the crowd. My brain convincing me that this was plausible. Only actually proving myself wrong by later doing it in periods of sobriety. I'd later ignore pre booked gigs, because I was too drunk to work.

I don't know the quantity of how much we were both drinking at the time; however, I know I spent around £10,000 between January, February and half of March.

I remember the day I admitted to my Alcoholism, I was tired and fed up. I was completely helpless by this point. I was truly an addict, co-depended, alcohol dependent alcoholic and I'd not even hit my rock bottom by this point. Little did I know what was still left as Holgate would later teach me.

Alcohol at this point controlled me completely. I'd lost all sense of control, maybe that's why I allowed myself to fall further with a narcissist, they have an incessive need to control, I had a need to be controlled, as I couldn't do it myself.

I lost all hope, any ability to even function as a normal human being.

By the end of the month, the spare room was full of empty bottles. So many empty bottles. I did admit my failings and shown them to my ex-wife begging for help. Hours, Days, Months it taken to clear all the empties from that house.

I remember reaching out feeling terrible, frightened and afraid. I just thought of myself as an alcoholic and just assumed I'd die this way. Looking back at this a year later, I didn't think the road to recovery would be this long. I thought a dry out at a&e and that's it. Oh, how very wrong I was to be so naive.

Now I know why I went to Rehab, to get better and begin my journey of recovery.

I am that far gone in my addiction it has ultimately progressed that far It's completely chronic. Tapering and cutting down doesn't work for me anymore. I can't stop, myself when I start. I have zero self-control over drinking anymore.

I did attend Chapman Barker Unit, Prestwich for a seven-day Radar Referral. I came out being nine days sober. I was told by my local service I would get an emergency rehab placement. An emergency bed in an emergency rehab. However, the person in charge of my funding application, looked at my blood results and apparently, I wasn't ever poorly enough to qualify for this.

So, I was told to attended six weeks' worth of sessions withing my access service.

Well before they'd consider me to fund into rehab.

Holy shit, was I supposed to do now? I took my final refuge in the fellowship of alcoholic anonymous, I really tried to do my ninety meetings in ninety days. I got to two weeks, full of cravings and triggers and no real coping mechanisms. I tried to reach out on a Friday night. Nobody answered. I felt like nobody cared again. What did I care?

Again, fuck it button pressed. There I was back at my fathers with a bottle of whiskey,

Looking back at that night. I needed help, someone anyone. I was doing my best to not pick up the bottle. Looking back, I'd have done anything not to.

I was ashamed, I fell.

By the end of my drinking and being controlled by My Narcissist I'd given up on my physical appearance. What was the point in being presentable? People were asking why I looked so scruffy, Not the smart man they knew and loved. I honestly didn't care back then. I was in a controlled marriage, I was drinking. I'd given up., Now I look back I feel shame. I know how to look after myself!

During stays at my fathers, he'd try to reduce my alcohol intake. I remember getting angry, I was a grown man. I knew if I fell out with my father I'd be truly and completely alone.

So then came the hiding of the alcohol at my dad's I'd stock up whilst he'd go to Oldham, I'd order bottles off Uber Eat and put them in the spare room. He must have thought I had a very weak bladder.

It's true as they say a behaviour can stick with you. I felt awful at the time, why was I lying to the one person on this whole planet who gave an actual shit about me?

I had defiled his loving home with bullshit, deceit and sneaky behaviour.

I remember being in the bath one night, so lost, so afraid. I remember crying uncontrollably, Who was I? I'm not the man who'd I'd become. I was lost, broken, abused. I had no self-will, no will power, so vulnerable. I'd been humiliated and abused in my marriage; I'd ruined myself with alcohol. I had no way out. Maybe death was actually better at this point., I got myself so worked up that night.

I wasn't a shadow of my former self. My illusions had faded, I was nothing, nobody and with nobody. I was alone.

Finally, everybody had won but me… I was just Kieran, the alcoholic.

Towards the end of my drinking, I'd be sat in the cot bed. The Cot Bed on my father's living room floor. By this time, I had left my Ex-Wife. My Dad would go to Morrisons every morning to get me a bottle of Whiskey. He'd then have to hold that bottle to me, with a straw. All because of the shakes, I was shaking that much it became impossible to consume enough alcohol independently just to keep me from having a seizure. I would carry on unaided to finish the bottle and pass out. Only to reawaken later and repeat the same disgusting procedure.

I wish there was a word with more emphasis than powerless to describe how I felt at this time in my life. All I really recall is trying to drink every emotion I was feeling away. The pain, the heartache, the sadness, the sorrow. I had thoroughly thrown myself the world's biggest pity party.

I used to have it all. However, I'm getting divorced, I'm alone, I have nothing. I am homeless. All excuses I made to carry on with the utterly destructive behaviours.

My health was declining, I couldn't even look after my hygiene, how was I supposed to ever think I could manage with my physical health? I was irritable, agitated all the time. I had no motivation.

I honest to god was so disappointed in myself and the way my poor father was having to look after me, I saw my physical health declining. My emotional and mental health. I put far too much on an elderly man. I put on too much, and more again knowing he couldn't take it. I was just selfish.

On my last detox, my final detox. I got diagnosed with a fatty liver and an enlarged spleen. I nearly popped a varicose. Which caused massive blood loss.

I was told by a doctor; another binge could easily kill me now. I was also diagnosed with Hepatitis E, normally your body can naturally fight this, however due to the Alcohol Abuse my body couldn't.

All these ailments were the shock I needed to realise I need to get sober and remain abstinent. By any means. I need professional help.

Contributing from my marriage, I have had serious low self-esteem problems prior to recovery for a while, anything I did made it worst. I'm grateful I find myself attractive these days. All thanks to people even just complimenting my appearance I stand tall and proud,

I wish I had the right people around me at the start of my recovery, I can only imagine what position I'd be in now.

I'd been on anti-depressants for years, again trying to balance out my system from all the heavy alcohol intake. As I write this page, I have been off anti-depressants for three months now, I honest explain the difference in how much more productive I am during my days now because of not being numbed out.

So that's it, there's only a handful of examples of the dark road my depression, alcoholism, abuse, heartbreak and trauma has taken me, I used these examples from my step one work in Holgate House, there was fifty pages of them. There's a lot less now, I've taken out so many examples that are either no longer relevant or important.

I've taken so much out of the breakdown of my marriage, the secret drinking, the drug use. I think you may already have the picture.

I of course, take account every day the things I'm conscious I still need to work on, abuse, getting raped. Losing myself, working on my confidence and self-esteem,

Alcoholism is a slippery road from that first to last taste.

Looking back on my past addiction, I feel an overwhelming sense of regret, sorrow, pain, and disappointment in myself.

My addiction had consumed me, and it led me to do things that I never thought I was capable of doing. I misbehaved, hurt others, and lost everything that was important to me. At the time, I thought I was in control of my addiction, but I was wrong. It controlled me, and I made choices that were damaging not only to myself but to those around me.

I neglected my responsibilities, lied to my loved ones, and hurt the people who cared about me the most.
Now that I am in recovery, I can see the full extent of the damage that my addiction caused. I have lost relationships, job opportunities, and a sense of self-worth.

It is painful to think about all the things that I could have done differently, and the opportunities that I missed out on. The regret and disappointment that I feel are sometimes overwhelming and they rot in the pits of my stomach.

I wish I could turn back time and make different choices, but I know that I can't. All I can do now is try to make amends, work on my recovery, and move forward in a positive direction.
It is a difficult road, but I know that it is possible to rebuild my life and regain the trust of those I have hurt

I have to learn from my mistakes, take responsibility for my actions, and strive to be a better person every day. It won't be easy, but I know that it is worth it to regain my sense of self-worth and rebuild my life.

9. KIERAN'S STORY

Here it is. The hardest story I must share with you.
It's the story of me, how I overcame every obstacle thrown at me.
How I stand naked before you with a soul to bare and a story to share.

Many people believe that addiction is solely a result of a traumatic or abusive childhood, but the reality is that addiction can affect anyone regardless of their upbringing. While it's true that childhood trauma can contribute to addiction, it's not the only factor.

Addiction is a complex disease that is influenced by a wide range of factors, including genetics, environment, mental health, and social and economic status.

While a supportive and loving family can reduce the risk of addiction, it's not a guarantee.

Even those like myself who came from stable and loving home can still be impacted by addiction. There are a variety of reasons why someone might turn to drugs or alcohol, including stress, peer pressure, and a desire to fit in.

The point I am trying to make is that addiction can affect anyone, regardless of their upbringing. We must not fall into the trap of assuming that addiction is solely a result of a traumatic childhood. Doing so only stigmatises those who are struggling with addiction and makes it harder for them to seek help.

Instead, we need to focus on supporting those who are struggling with addiction, regardless of their background. We must ensure that resources are available for those who need them and that we're doing everything we can to reduce the stigma associated with addiction.

I started young in addiction, although I wasn't an addict the behaviours was there.
I have lied, I have manipulated, been dishonest, disloyal. I have betrayed trust. I have been a fool. In my younger and formative years.

I always strived to be better. To be more, want more and need more.
Now I humbly ask for your forgiveness. I wasn't the man I knew I was deep inside.

I was a projection of what a person should be, just with quirks and ambition.
True ambition really set upon me, moving on and starting a business that would eventually undo me.
It would show me the true darkness of a man, one who would eventually go on to be fundamentally unhappy for the next couple of years to come.

I make no excuses and pass no blame for my addiction. It's mine, nobody could have foreseen it. Nobody could have stopped it. A true friend has taught me you can't deprive somebody of their rock bottom.
Rock bottom hit me hard, it hit me with a trauma bond. I was nothing. There was nothing of me left. Only a man who would find discomfort in the bottom of a whiskey bottle.
When I realised, I had finally gone too far, I couldn't stop. I went further down and got hurt more in the process. Suddenly everything I had worked for was pointless, what's the point?

The number of times I'd triggered in early recovery and relapsed, knowing that the right care wasn't there for me. The services on offer to Alcoholics in the community are sub-standard. I reached and fought out everywhere I could to get help and support. Eventually I was left alone, broken, suicidal, homeless and addicted.

The people who were true to me, and there through the thick of it, regardless of me; my circumstances and fought with me have become my world. The people who stood tall and proud with me at my lowest. I will not forget. I can't thank these people enough. Those who didn't it's their loss.
I really had hit rock bottom. You have already read what my addiction and my addictive behaviours had led me to.

To a man I shouldn't have ever become.

Today, I am me, unconditionally, unapologetically and graciously me. Ambition isn't a unit of measurement anymore. Ambition is smiling in the morning. Ambition is being content. Those are the things I now thrive towards.
I'm so grateful for the people that helped me, stood up for me and forgave me when I couldn't even forgive myself. To you I thank you again!

I couldn't do this on my own. I now reach out to the best recovery network there is.
This is it. It is the story of me, I don't apologise if you don't like everything you read, it's my story and my survival.

Addiction, betrayal, deceit and powerlessness ravished my body, my mind and my soul.
I stand as this man today different. I never knew how different I would be.
I have done things I am really not proud of, and I have made amends where possible. I am also conscious of my shortcomings and intend to improve on them.

I cast my mind back often to my last and final detox, the worst and the last one. I actually begged for death. I wanted deaths warm embrace, to take me into its warmth. To free me of all the pain I was feeling, the emotional agony I was trapped in. The vicious cycle of Alcoholism. The betrayal of everything.
To be lay in a bed unable to move unless you're shaking, sweating or vomiting begging for death is really the rock bottom.

They teach you in Rehab, the yet to come. The things your yet to loose, I'd had lost everything but my life. Yet I was begging someone to take this from me. The disease had ravished my body through and through, it spat me out, with me wanting

life to end. That's not being suicidal. Its having enough, of everything.
Don't get me wrong Alcohol is no game. Especially one I wished I never had played. It was the end of me.

The start of me I have now was always within me, Just because my life is better now than it ever has been has nothing to do with my sobriety. It was always within me. It took being clean to unlock it. I contribute no present attributes to the addiction.
However, I'm grateful for every day.

Withdrawal is the most exhausting and frightening place a person can be, the sweating, shaking, vomiting, the delirium tremors. Please be warned.

There's one thing that I don't really mention to be honest and that was getting my ADHD diagnosis last year.
For me it wasn't a diagnosis. It was an explanation.
An explanation to why I don't think the same as everybody else, why I'm "quirky"
However, the one thing that it did give me more than anything was relief. That I'm not alone and so what if the world is black and white. Or I started decorating now I'm renovating back from brick.

It's a part of me, my make up.
It's also showing true god damn strength. Do you know how hard it has been for thirty years, knowing there's something off with you but shrinking yourself to fit in? Altering yourself, to be somebody else's view of a person or man? I know now that if people don't accept the loveable friendly bloke I actually am, well they're not living in my life rent free.

I've never had so much relief as the past year, and probably play the ADHD card far too much and all too often. However just another reason why I'm me.

Today I am still working on my past trauma, the time I was raped, and the Police failed me. The services which were there to help, they failed me.

I remember what it was like to wake up every morning with a heavy feeling in my chest. It was like there was a weight sitting on top of me, crushing me down into the mattress. I'd try to shake it off, but it was always there, a constant reminder of the demon that lived inside me.

It's something that I carried with me for as long as I can remember. It's the ghost of my past, the shadow that followed me wherever I go. It's the memories that I try to forget, the nightmares that keep me up at night.

It's hard to explain what it's like to deal with a demon. It's like there was a battle going on inside of me, a constant struggle between the light and the darkness. Sometimes I felt like I'm winning, like I was in control. But then there are moments when the demon takes over, when it feels like there's no escape.

It's the little things that used to trigger it, the memories that come flooding back when I least expected it to. It was the smell of the perfume she used to wear, the sound of a certain song, the taste of a particular food.

It's like my brain was wired to make those connections, to take me back to a time that I didn't want to remember. And when that happened, it was like I was transported back in time. Even now there are times I can feel the fear, the anger, the pain. It's like I'm living it all over again. And then the demon takes over, filling me with a sense of despair and hopelessness.

It's a constant battle, one that I fight every single day. But I'm learning to cope, to find ways to keep the demon at bay. It's not easy, and there are days when I feel like I'm losing the fight. But I know that I can't give up, that I have to keep pushing forward.
Because the demon may live inside me, but it doesn't define me. I am more than my past, more than the memories that haunt me. I am strong, and I will keep fighting, no matter how hard it gets.

One thing I have learnt from my own story, sometimes it's ok, just not to be okay. Some days are just bad! That's a fact.

However, when you're on a program of recovery, you are productive. I don't sit still anymore. I haven't watched television in months. I'm rarely on my phone. I live. I don't just live for the day. I live for my life. My days are so much better.

Once you find you have something to protect like a life you have built, you'll surely do anything to protect it. I worked hard, to recover. To accept myself, to be myself and to really love myself.

Nobody and nothing will ever be allowed to take that away from me again.

Not every day I have now is smiles and butterflies, most days are attributed to the most amazing person that has ever existed, who truly is my, my twin, I cannot tell you how strong of a person it takes to say they want to be with you forever and mean it. Then to show you every day. That they see past your flaws, that would never get weaponised against you.

This amazing human being picked up the pieces of me I didn't even know needing picking up.
All I can say is thank you as well.

Surprising it was late 2022, aged 30 when I finally got my diagnosis for ADHD. It explained so much, the reasons I am the way I am, the way I am. My poor partner, had to accept their ADHDer rather quickly, they taught themself all about it, They forgives the quirks and I think they secretly like them.

Recovery for me was the biggest journey I ever embarked on. It has been long, with more bumps in the road than on a former Friday night,

I have found myself, a true representation of the real person within, I'm happy. I didn't think that would ever be possible. However, this hard work has to start within, You can't bed or wish it to happen, you have to work hard. You have to take a long look at a mirror in front of you.

It's a very yucky process. You have to visit the demons with in, have tea with them. Then fight them unarmed. I suppose the best way I can describe it, Is going on to the boss level on a video game. You have to bring your all, your 100%.

You have to be prepared to visit the depths of your soul. Memories that you were never wanting to visit have to be cleansed.

You'll need humility, You have to admit your wrong doings. Only by cast a light on us can we see ourselves for who we really are, It wasn't easy.

It's very easy for people to say, well done you've. Taken the first step. That's the easy part. The next step gets harder, and you will feel like it will never end, It gets harder, and suddenly it becomes easy.

When I look back on my life, I can hardly recognise the person I used to be. I was trapped in a cycle of alcoholism and domestic abuse that seemed like it would never end. But now, after months of hard work, I'm proud to say that I'm recovered from both.

It wasn't easy, of course. I had to face some hard truths about myself and my life. I had to admit that I had a problem with alcohol, and that my partner's behaviour towards me was abusive. It took a long time for me to build up the courage to leave that relationship and seek help, but I knew that I had to do it if I wanted to get better.

I was an addict I was in dark and difficult time in my life. It caused me to neglect my responsibilities, lose my business, and most tragically, damage the relationships I had with my family. I was so consumed by my addiction that I didn't realise the harm I was causing to those who loved me the most.

I remember the pain and disappointment in my family's eyes when they realised the extent of my addiction. They tried everything to help me, but I was so deep into my addiction that I couldn't see the damage I was causing.
It wasn't until I hit rock bottom that I realised. I sought help and began the long and difficult journey towards sobriety.

It wasn't easy, and there were times when I relapsed, but I never gave up.
It took a lot of time and effort, but eventually, I managed to rebuild my relationship with my family. There were a lot of tears shed, but they were willing to forgive me and support me on my journey towards recovery.

I am forever grateful for the second chance they gave me. I regret the pain and hurt I caused them during my addiction, but I am proud of the person I have become in sobriety.

I never take their forgiveness and support for granted, and I am constantly working on being the best version of myself. Rebuilding my relationship with my family was one of the hardest things I have ever had to do, but it was also one of the most rewarding.

It taught me the value of forgiveness and the importance of showing up for those who love you.
I'm amazed I got the opportunity to rebuild my relationship with my family and will always cherish the second chance they gave me. I am now living a sober and fulfilling life, and I owe it all to the love and support of my family.

Recovering from alcoholism was a difficult process. I had to learn how to cope with my emotions in healthy ways instead of relying on alcohol to numb the pain. I went to therapy, attended support groups, and took steps to make sure that I wasn't putting myself in situations where I might be tempted to drink. It wasn't always easy, but with time, it got easier.

Recovering from domestic abuse was even harder. I had to learn how to rebuild my self-esteem and trust in other people. I had to deal with the trauma that I had experienced and learn how to set boundaries to protect myself from further harm. I had to work hard to relearn what a healthy relationship looks like, and to recognise the warning signs of abuse so that I wouldn't fall into the same pattern again.

Being belittled by a spouse can be an incredibly isolating and lonely experience. When someone you love and trust treats you with contempt or dismisses your feelings and opinions, it can leave you feeling devalued and alone.

Belittlement can take many forms, including verbal abuse, criticism, and ridicule. It can erode your self-esteem and confidence, leaving you feeling unworthy of love and companionship.

When this behaviour comes from a spouse, it can be particularly devastating, as marriage is supposed to be a partnership built on mutual respect and support.
Being in a relationship with someone who belittles you can also create a sense of isolation, as you may feel as though you can't talk to anyone about what you're going through. You may fear that others will judge you or dismiss your concerns, or you may simply feel too ashamed to reach out for help. Over time, this sense of loneliness can become all-encompassing, affecting not only your marriage but also your relationships with friends and family. You may withdraw from social situations, avoid seeking help, and even become depressed or anxious.

It is important to recognise that belittlement is a form of emotional abuse and should never be tolerated in a marriage or any relationship. If you are experiencing this type of behaviour from a spouse or partner, it is important to seek help and support from trusted friends, family, or professionals. No one deserves to feel isolated or alone in their relationship.

But despite the challenges, I'm proud of how far I've come. I'm sober, and I'm no longer in an abusive relationship. I'm surrounded by a supportive community of friends and family who love and care about me. I know that I still have work to do, and that recovery is a lifelong process, but I'm grateful for the progress I've made so far.

Recovering from alcoholism and domestic abuse has taught me that it's never too late to change your life. It's not easy, and it's not always comfortable, but it's worth it.

If you or someone you know is struggling with these issues, know that there is help and support available. You don't have to go through this alone.

My favourite moment in recovery was the night I realised the obsession had lifted. I was on a dance floor, dancing! Sober! Not a single thought of alcohol, I took no notice.
The obsession had gone. I was free.

If you're honestly serious about a programme, it does work if you work it. So, work it your worth it.

The story keeps going, just remember some characters are never worth revisiting. Some heroes don't come in till later on in the story. Sometimes the hero was there all along.
If you have been there for me and are still there for me. You're my hero. Thank you

My biggest surprise was finding true love.

True love is a powerful force that can bring happiness, fulfilment, and meaning to our lives.

It goes beyond just physical attraction or infatuation and involves a deep emotional connection with someone who understands us on a profound level.

One of the key aspects of true love is the recognition of the qualities that make a good person. When we are truly in love, we see the best in our partner, and we appreciate the things that make them kind, caring, and compassionate. We notice the little things, like the way they always put us first or the way they show us attention and affection.

A person who truly loves us will be there for us through thick and thin. They will stand by us, even when things get tough, and offer support, comfort, and understanding. They will be our biggest cheerleader, celebrating our successes and helping us navigate the challenges that life throws our way.

In a truly loving relationship, there is a sense of mutual respect and trust. We feel comfortable being our true selves around our partner, knowing that they accept us for who we are, flaws and all. We communicate openly and honestly, sharing our thoughts, fears, and dreams with each other. True love involves a deep emotional connection that goes beyond just physical attraction. We are drawn to our partner's personality, values, and beliefs, and we appreciate the unique qualities that make them who they are.

Ultimately, true love is about finding someone who loves us unconditionally, who sees the best in us, and who is committed to supporting us through all of life's ups and downs.

It is a bond that is built on trust, respect, and a deep emotional connection, and it has the power to transform our lives in ways that we never thought possible.
A quote to end,

Just remember, sobriety, recovery and abstinence isn't a destination. It's a journey. The best journey you could embark on.

10. QUOTES ABOUT REBUILDING

FINDING MYSELF

Holgate house, my friend, where have you been?

Getting back to me, I've never been so keen.

I've changed my clothes I wear

I now dress with pride and care.

I'm starting to look like me again,

My thoughts are back to sane.

I've even dyed my hair a time or two,

Holgate house, I own my pride thanks to you.

I've been eating well,

Round the stomach time will tell.

I'm even planning my parting gift,

Cause Holgate House, my spirits you really did lift.

I have hope and a future now.

Stand tall and take a well-deserved bow.

Cause without you my friend

I know how quickly my life would end.

You are rebuilding my strength

For my hope I know you've gone the length

For now, I must go to bed,

Without you Holgate I'd be dead.

INSPIRATION

You're the perfect fit for your inspiration

Just make sure that inspiration comes from within

TODAY

Last year you said next year,

Last month you said next month,

Yesterday you said tomorrow,

Words are just words until you take action.

So, start today.

I AM WORTHY

Most of my life has been spent trying to shrink myself. Trying to become smaller. Quieter. Less sensitive. Less opinionated. Less needy. Because I didn't want to be a burden. I didn't want to be too much or push people away. I wanted people to like me. I wanted to be cared for and valued. I wanted to be wanted. So, for years, I sacrificed myself for the sake of making other people happy. For years, I suffered. But I'm tired of suffering, and I'm done shrinking. It's not my job to change who I am in order to become someone else's idea of a worthwhile human being.

I am worthwhile.

Not because other people think I am, but because I exist, and therefore I matter.

My thoughts matter. My feelings matter. My voice matters and with or without anyone's permission or approval, I will continue to be who I am and speak my truth.

Even if it makes people angry. Even if it makes them uncomfortable. Even if they choose to leave. I refuse to shrink. I choose to take up space. I choose to honour my feelings. I choose to give myself permission to get my needs met.

Finally. I CHOOSE ME!

WHOLESOME

I walked through the valleys and the depths of my inner self, looking for a monster that was expressing its hell. I entered a room and standing before me was only my shadow crying for help. I took it by the hand and let it walk out with me, knowing only love could set the pain free. Now my shadow was set free. I let it go. I allowed it to leave me. Now I'm quite like the night, content; I am whole.

GROWING

I grew from the things that have tried to destroy me.

It's been beautiful to grow again, to begin again.

I'm so different in the space of a couple of weeks.

I can feel myself becoming the man I was destined to be.
Even if it has involved a shopping spree.

Letting go of old Kieran was the best decision I ever made.
No longer shrinking myself and being true to my feelings and
wants. I just can't describe the ecstasy of how good things are
going for me.

Onwards and upwards still!

I've only just started my journey and I look forward to seeing
where my next step takes me.

TIME TO REGENERATE

If the Doctor can regenerate, then why can't I?

That's what I'm going to do. Regenerate myself.

Listening to all the last words of each Doctor got me thinking, what would my words be?

I might not have been perfect, but I had fun.

I got my heart broken, I got myself in a mess, but I got myself out of it. I learned to never change for anyone but for myself. Every day is a new day, a new day to smile. Don't let anybody take away your smile.

Old Kieran… I let you go.

Right then, Kieran whoever I'm about to be. Tag! You're it.

A NEW BEGINNING

So, it begins. I'm on my way to my new life.

I've made peace with letting go.

You can't change your past, but you can deal with it and move on.

You can start a fresh.

Hello new Kieran. I'm honestly so excited.

How many people get this opportunity to begin again? I don't intend to waste a second of it.

KIERAN V2.0

I think this is the most important thing I've ever had the complete pleasure to write.

Hello, Kieran, V2.0!

I did it. I dealt with my inner demons.

I got lost a time or two but here I am on the other side.

I've made peace where there was pain. I've made examples of what I will and not deal with in a healthy way. I've also decided what I want in my life.

I'm home!

I honestly can't tell you how much of a different man I am today.

It gives me such warmth knowing I'm supported and surrounded by amazing people, friends, family and my other family (The friends that I should have been related to)

I personally want to thank everyone who's been there for me this past 12 months whilst I got my shit together.

Was it easy? Absolutely not. However, I asked life why aren't you easy?

Life's response? Cause people don't appreciate easy.

I can honestly say after being fundamentally unhappy for many years, I have found true happiness. True happiness is waking up in the morning, smiling at yourself in the mirror, it's the first cup of coffee you sip. It's not keeping yourself occupied for the sake of it. It's taking a day and making it your own.

To think this time last year when I realised, I had a problem with Alcohol. It's been a long year since.

However, I've done everything I could to get better and I can finally say I did it.

I don't have to wear a fake smile and say I'm fine.

I have a genuine warm face with a can-do attitude.

I regenerated with a new style, new ambitions, new sense of achievement and more importantly. A newfound relief and appreciation for peace.

If anyone on the earth can tell you, don't be afraid. Just take that first step. It's me.

COMEBACK

Let's talk about your comeback.

All the times you fell and got back up.

Let's talk about the lessons. All the hurt you turned into healing. Let's talk about the version of you that you haven't met yet, and all the versions of you that helped you get to where you are now.

Let's talk about your survival, all the things that were sent to break you, and you barely even flinched. Let's talk about how beautiful it is that the ugliest parts of your story are what taught you grace. Let's talk about all of the times you doubted yourself, how you used the pieces of those moments to build yourself back up into the most certain thing you've ever known. You dove straight into the chaos and came out holding nothing, but peace. You, unbreakable beauty, strong and fierce and brave, I see you and every version of you that carried you here. I see all of you.

Let's talk about how far you've come and how you're still standing.

SELF LOVE

I will not apologise for choosing myself this time.

Self-love is the chapter, I always wanted to write

ADHD

Finally, a diagnosis, why my world is black and white.

Why it can appear as though I don't give a shite.

I'm not strange, weird or show hostility.

I just have a unique super ability.

I now love to hyper focus and dive right in.

Even though I most will probably pack it in.

I'm surprised it taken so long to figure it out,

My diagnosis just shouting like a ticket tout.

I'm finding it fun, fun to be around,

Even if it's making me act like a clown.,

WORKING ON SHORTCOMINGS

You may not of wanted an outcome that occurred.

In your situation although we aren't always in control, or we get so caught up in our feelings and emotions that we don't think things out first ending in decisions which are soon held in the most prestigious decisions we've made.

Once again, it's an honest display of our humanity on show.

It really shows that we are always incapable of making the right decisions or choices straight off the bat.

As I'm so conscious daily to accept, understand and stringently work on my short comings.

I find it important for me to understand that you can leave the past where it belongs.

However just because it may be present in your present doesn't mean it's the future of your future. You can easily take the steps to make sure it isn't.

NEW START

I don't give a shit about proving my goodness to anyone, because I no longer care about being perceived as good. If you need me to be a villain in your story, that's fine. If you need me to be an angel in your story, that's fine too. Your story has no bearing on my truest nature.

Not everyone deserved to know me, to touch the pieces I so freely offered before I knew that knowing me is a privilege, my time, my heart, my trust.

But I don't regret it. I don't they we should ever regret a trust fall. Maybe they needed those pieces of me. Maybe they learned something. I know I did.

The ruining of me was the birth of me and all this chaos was not in vain.

When I speak about knowing my worth, it's not coming from a place of ego or arrogance. I stand by my positive attributes with conviction, but the difference is I'm conscious of my shortfalls and work on them every day.

When somebody holds a space in my heart, there is nothing I wouldn't do for them. Generosity, patience, and loyalty are traits of mine cherished dearly by those who know me. But I won't pretend other emotions don't consume me. Because they do. However, it is my unwavering devotion to give the positivity inside me a stronger voice-one which overrides all. When I say I know my worth, it's because I've done the work to get here. It's because I continue doing so. I know what I have to offer, and I stand strong in that fact alone.

DISCOVERY

I think the best thing I ever did in my adult life was start digging deep and asking myself why I am the way I am and do things the way I do. It takes a ton of work and intentionality but getting to know yourself on a deeper level will help you thrive.

SELF IMPROVEMENT

Once you start seeing the results of self-improvement, it really becomes addicting. You start falling in love with the person you're becoming, the places you're going, the things you're doing, & it motivates you to work even harder

SOME DAYS

Some days are sad guy days (extra time in bed, hot showers, burning candles, warm tea). Other days are bad boy days (loud music, favourite outfits, lots of productivity).

Both are important. Both are necessary. Don't be afraid to listen to what you need.

LEAVE IT IN YOUR PAST

I usually become a ghost to those who no longer deserve my time. I've never seen a point in explaining my absence to someone who failed to appreciate my presence.

You don't owe any explanations to those who hurt you.

THAT BROKEN YEAR

There was that broken year, on that broken road, with that broken me, and thank goodness I'm not on that road anymore, but still I reminisce sometimes to remind myself what roads not to take, the lessons from my mistakes, and most of all, how far I've come since this time last year.

PEACE

The peace I have now was worth everything I lost.

START LIVING, IT'S TIME

Get out of your head and back on your feet. Remember who the hell you are.

This means returning to your body because you're missing your life living in your thoughts.

Feel the ground beneath your feet and start living. It's time.

FIND YOURSELF

Be young, go find yourself. Go to a distant land alone. Let go of that rucksack of everything you've been carrying.

Go and let go.

Return home, return better for it.

Return wiser, smarter and stronger.

Don't look back in several years and have a single regret.

WHEN I LOVED MYSELF ENOUGH

When I loved myself enough, I stopped allowing people to hurt my heart. I stopped making excuses for their bad behaviour. I stopped putting everyone before me. When I loved myself enough, I started saying no to people and things that didn't align with my soul. I started to put healthy boundaries in place. I started to talk kindly to myself.
When I loved myself enough, I stopped being a victim and I started to live in my power.
When I loved myself enough.

PICKING UP THE PIECES

I think the nicest compliment I've had in recovery is "It's nice to meet you Kieran"
A genuinely heart felt compliment from someone who cared, who's watched me grow.

From the rock bottom nobody could have deprived me from. To hear how unrecognisable I am, means a great deal, it's me reflecting, I'm so productive now. I'm turning a house into a home, I'm out socialising and enjoying myself. I am making time for those that matter most to me.

I can feel the confidence back in me, I'm assertive to my needs, I look the way I feel on the inside.
After being so destroyed, low, deprived of being valued, to have them things again from within is something I simply refuse to take for granted.
I have my social life back, I get to be the life and soul again, the funny, cheeky chap. Only with a story to tell and a future to be enjoyed.

After my make over I actually feel attractive again! Not just in looks, but like I'm worth something once more.
Life is just so good, healing, growing and adjusting.
Yet I've just driven down the motorway singing my head off.
Life's good when you allow it to be.
Life's good when you have reasons to smile.

When someone loves you enough to hold you that close, to let you in to their hurt and their history so you know they truly are with you and understand you. It's amazing

NEW REALITY

You're entering a new reality where everything will start to go your way.
It's time. You had enough lessons.
You did the work. You overcame so much. You believed even when it was hard to. You never gave up. You pushed through it all. Now it's your turn to receive in a major way.

RUN AWAY

I used to be so good at running away.
That never helped anyone, me or a situation.

Finally, I'm at that point in my life where I'm no longer needing to run from anything. I'm simply enjoying all opportunities offered to me.

I made a conscious decision, I don't survive in my life, my recovery and my day.
I live in my life; I enjoy my life.
I love being me

REBUILD

Rebuilding your life after addiction is not just about getting sober, it's about creating a new life for yourself. It's about discovering who you are without the crutch of drugs or alcohol and learning to love that person.

It's about finding purpose and meaning in your life and building a future that you can be proud of.

RECREATE

Recreating your life after addiction is not easy, but it is worth it. It's about taking responsibility for your actions and making a commitment to yourself to live a better life.

It's about facing your fears and confronting the issues that led to your addiction.

It's about learning to love yourself again and building a life that is filled with purpose, meaning, and happiness.

JUST FOR TODAY PT2

Just for today I will remember and remind myself I am not my addiction, and my addiction is not me.

GRADUATION

You've done the lessons; you've done the hard work.

You've studied your disease.

You know what you're up against now Kieran. just remember, it will always be there. don't let it pull you back

WELCOME HOME

I left my home with a heavy heart,
A victim of addiction's deadly art,

My mind and soul were torn apart,
And I knew I had to make a fresh start.

I journeyed far to seek my cure,
To break the chains and find pure,

And in the midst of pain and fear,
I found a hope that drew me near.

The journey was long, the road was rough,
But the light that shone was bright enough,

To guide me through the darkest hour,
And help me find a place of power.

Now I'm back, my heart is light,
My eyes are clear, my future bright,

I'm home, where I belong,
And I know I'll never go wrong.

I'm filled with joy, and peace, and love,
And I thank the Lord, the One above,

For guiding me along the way,

And bringing me home, to stay.

So now I raise my voice in song,
And shout my thanks, all day long,

For the journey that led me here,
And the love that helped me conquer fear.

SECRET THERAPIST

A secret therapist came to me,
In moments when I couldn't see,

A light to guide me through the night,
And give me strength to win the fight.

They listened with a heart of gold,
And gently helped my story unfold,

They knew my pain, They knew my strife,
And gave me hope to rebuild my life.

We met in secret, in a sacred space,
A place of healing, a safe embrace,

And there I found the courage to be,
The person I was meant to be.

They helped me face my darkest fears,
And wipe away my falling tears,

They gave me tools to heal my heart,
And helped me make a brand-new start.

With their guidance, I found my way,
And slowly learned to live each day.

With strength and courage, and a heart renewed,
And a sense of purpose, bright and true.

So, here's to the secret therapist,
The one who helped me heal and persist,

Thank you for being by my side,
And helping me reclaim my pride.

11. QUOTES ABOUT FALLING IN LOVE

IMAGINE

Imagine being in a relationship where the only thing keeping you from each other is work.

You spend most of the day looking forward to 5pm so you can haul ass home to them.

UNCONDITIONAL

I think I would love you even at your worst.
Even when you didn't love yourself.
With tears in your eyes, feeling not quite good enough.
I would still love you.
I would still adore every single tiny piece of who you are.
And to me you would still be everything I've ever wanted.

LOVE AIN'T EASY

Loving somebody is not easy, especially when they have dusty cobwebs hung like decorations off their heartstrings and they believe the creases around their eyes are there to catch fallen tears, completely forgetting that they were formed by smiling too wide.

Loving somebody is not easy, but it should never be a chore that you must drag your feet to continue, it is not that last shot of vodka that finally spreads your body with warmth. Loving somebody is staying up too late and watching the sun dance into the sky, knowing you will hurt from fatigue the next day but understanding that sometimes beautiful things are worth it.

Loving somebody is a prayer your veins sing and a headfirst dive into arctic water, sending your body into infinite shock. I looked into your eyes and saw songbirds and they told me I was allowed to be happy

Loving someone is knowing you are not the first love, but you could be their last love. Loving someone is accepting them for who they truly are. No matter what they've been through.

Love isn't all flowers, dancing and kissing. Love is looking at someone and knowing not only are you home, but you'd be home wherever they are.

Love is them telling you to take yourself to a forest to write the book that's going to hopefully one day save a life,

Love isn't selfish.

Love is precious.,

I found love, Not just any love,

I found everlasting love.

YOUR EYES

Looking into your eyes, It's like I can't breathe. It's like all the oxygen I once knew as good was taken from my body. Your essence completely consumes me and my being, I can feel the vibrations through the floorboards, Your eyes tell a million stories I can hear the echoes in the wind., however our happy ever after is the one I want to listen to again and again.

HUMOUR

Two people, with a dark sense of humour
Laughing at the absurdities of life
Finding joy in the macabre and the morbid
Their laughter a sign of a shared strife
They see the world through twisted eyes
Where tragedy and comedy collide
A world where death is just a punchline
And laughter is a way to survive
They revel in the darkest of jokes
Finding humour in the most taboo
Their laughter echoes in the silence
A bond that only they can renew
The world may see them as strange
Their humour may seem twisted and grim
But in each other's company, they find solace
Two kindred spirits, sharing a whimsical whim
So let them laugh at death and darkness
For in their laughter, they find light
Two people with a shared sense of humour
A bond that shines bright, even in the darkest night.

FALLING IN LOVE WITH YOU

Falling in love with you was like being struck by lightning - intense, electrifying, and impossible to forget.
You make my heart race and my soul sing - falling in love with you has been the most intense experience of my life.
From the moment I met you, I knew I was in trouble - I was falling in love with you, and there was no stopping it.
Falling in love with you was like being caught in a whirlwind - a wild, exhilarating, and unforgettable experience.
I never knew that falling in love could be so intense and overwhelming - with you, my heart is on fire.
Falling in love with you was like diving into a deep ocean - a rush of emotions and sensations that took my breath away.
I'm addicted to the feeling of falling in love with you - it's the most intense, beautiful thing I've ever experienced.
Falling in love with you was like a rollercoaster ride - full of twists and turns, ups and downs, but always thrilling.
You make me feel alive in a way I never knew was possible - falling in love with you has been the most intense and wonderful journey.
Falling in love with you was like discovering a whole new world - a place of magic, wonder, and endless possibilities.

BROKEN

Sometimes, two souls can find each other, two sous that are fundamentally broken, they can find each other in the time of healing. They use that time to connect as soul mates. The connect in ways that only movies could dream of. The light a spark and passion more intense than any feeling one person has the euphoric receptors to handle.

They appreciate everything from each other's life lessons. *That's truth, That's love.*

HOW ON EARTH

You know I come with big red warning triangles? Alarm bells that should be ringing in your ears.

Wait you find me attractive? Are you blind?

You think I look nice?

You won't leave me?

You love me?

You love me unconditionally?

I know broken souls are supposed to find each other, yours is pure, yours is warm, I don't deserve you. Is what old me would say, thinking I was worthless.

Yet because of you I don't feel worthless anymore.

You mended them broken parts; the ones I didn't know that were even broken. You showed my soul is equally as beautiful to deserve you.

LOVE

I wanted to take a moment to express my deepest gratitude to you. I am so blessed to have you in my life, and I cannot thank you enough for loving me despite my obvious flaws.

Fortunately, you have never seen me at my worst – my moments of weakness, my lapses in judgment, my mistakes and missteps. Yet I know you would have stood by my side through it all, with unwavering love and support. You have shown me compassion and understanding when I needed it the most, and you have helped me to see the best in myself even when I couldn't.

I know that I am far from perfect, and I am keenly aware of my own imperfections. But your love has taught me that imperfection is not a weakness, but rather a strength. It is what makes us human, and what allows us to connect with one another on a deeper level.

Your love has shown me that true beauty lies not in flawless perfection, but in the imperfect, messy, and complicated parts of ourselves that make us who we are.

Your acceptance of my flaws has given me the courage to be vulnerable, to open up and share my deepest fears and insecurities with you, knowing that you will love me all the same.

I want you to know that I do not take your love for granted. I cherish every moment that we spend together, and I am

constantly in awe of your kindness, your grace, and your unwavering commitment to our relationship.
Thank you, from the bottom of my heart, for loving me despite my obvious flaws.

You are my rock, my anchor, and my soulmate, and I cannot imagine my life without you. I promise to love and cherish you for all the days of my life, and to be there for you in the same way that you have been there for me.

HER EYES

When I look into her eyes, I see the whole universe reflected back at me. It's like every star in the sky, every planet and every galaxy, all swirling together in a mesmerising dance of light and colour. In her eyes, I see the beauty and wonder of the cosmos, and the infinite possibilities that exist within it.

But it's not just the vastness of the universe that I see in her eyes - I also see the depth and complexity of the human experience.

I see the joys and sorrows, the hopes and fears, the triumphs and setbacks that make up the rich tapestry of life. I see the struggles and challenges that we all face, and the resilience and strength that it takes to overcome them.

When I look into her eyes, I see all of these things, and so much more. I see the essence of who she is - her soul, her spirit, her very being - laid bare before me. And I feel grateful and humbled to be able to share in this incredible experience with her.

UNIVERSE

For me, seeing the whole universe in someone's eyes is not just a poetic metaphor - it's a powerful and deeply transformative experience. It reminds me of the vastness and wonder of the world around us, and the limitless potential that exists within each and every one of us. And it inspires me to be a better person, to strive for greatness, and to always keep reaching for the stars.

HONESTY

Falling in love with someone who values honesty is a beautiful thing. It means you can be your authentic self and know that you are loved for who you truly are.

DEEP IN LOVE

Love is not just a feeling, it's an all-consuming force that ignites every cell in my being. It's the warmth of the sun on my skin, the rush of adrenaline in my veins, and the beat of my heart. When I'm with you, every breath I take is filled with the intensity of this love - a love that transcends time, distance, and all obstacles. It's a love that makes me feel alive, and I am forever grateful to have you by my side, my heart intertwined with yours in an unbreakable bond

12. FALLING IN LOVE FOR THE LAST TIME

There was a time in my life when I never wanted to fall in love again. I had experienced the pain and trauma of being in a relationship with a narcissist and had suffered from domestic abuse. The experience had left me feeling broken and shattered, and I never wanted to put myself through that kind of pain again.

I remember feeling so hurt and betrayed, wondering how someone who claimed to love me could treat me so poorly. I had never experienced such intense emotions before, and I couldn't shake the feeling that I was somehow responsible for what had happened.

For a long time, I closed myself off from the world. I never wanted to kiss another stranger or be with anyone again.

The thought of dating was terrifying, and I couldn't imagine ever putting myself in that kind of vulnerable position again. But as time went on, I began to realise that my past experiences didn't have to define my future.

I started to seek help from a therapist and learned to recognise the signs of narcissistic behaviour and abuse. I began to heal, slowly but surely, and realised that falling in love again was possible.

It wasn't easy, and there were times when I struggled with my past experiences. But I began to understand that not all relationships are the same, and there are people out there who will love and respect me for who I am.

I started to dip my toes into the dating pool, taking things slowly and cautiously. I met some wonderful people, but I had to learn to trust again. It was a process, but eventually, I found someone who loved and respected me for who I was.

Since I was victim to narcissistic behaviour and domestic abuse it can be incredibly traumatic and leave lasting scars. It's natural to feel hesitant and scared about falling in love again.

But with time, patience, and the right support, it is possible to heal and find love again. It's essential to seek help and surround yourself with people who will support you on your journey to healing.

Signs of healing from something toxic? I remember the only time I ever tried to explain myself. I tried to reassure her that I

wouldn't ever fall off the wagon. I was just assuming she would no longer be present in my life if I fell.
First reaction, why would I leave you? Why would I let you deal with it on your own?
Wait, one second… you won't??
Positive and healthy started with I'd like to think I'd always be here and always would want to help.
That's understanding, that's peace.

In one point in my life, I didn't think I could change. For years, I was a slave to alcohol and domestic abuse. I didn't think I deserved any better. And the alcohol only made things worse.

Until one day I met her

She immediately started listening to the stories of me and what lead me to addiction and the battles that I faced to overcome it. I was struck by her beauty, but I didn't think I was worthy of her attention.

I never believed in love at first sight, but that all changed when I met her. We had an intense connection that I couldn't explain. It was like our souls recognised each other and we were drawn to each other in a way that was beyond physical attraction.
We were two of the same.

On the night of our first date, we went out for dinner and talked for hours about everything under the sun. It was like we had known each other for years. We laughed, we shared stories, and we connected on a deep level that I had never experienced before.

Our first kiss was something only ever written in a fairy-tale. It was electric. I felt a jolt of energy run through my body and I knew that this was going to ignite an ever so longing spark. We kissed for what seemed like hours, our bodies pressed together, our hands exploring every inch of each other.

I felt a sense of anticipation and excitement. Just from a kiss. We was going to be something spiritual, something that would change me forever.

And it was. our hearts beat as they were one. It was like we were in a trance, lost in the moment, lost in each other. It was the most intense physical, emotional, and spiritual connection I had ever experienced. I felt that it would be forever impossible to connect that emotionally with someone in just a kiss.

As the sun rose and the morning light filled the room, we lay in each other's arms, exhausted but content. I knew that this was just the beginning of our journey together. That we had a connection that was deeper than anything I had ever known. And as I looked her eyes, I knew that I was finally home .

As we continued to see each other, I began to realise that she accepted me for who I was. She didn't judge me for my past mistakes, my history or my struggles with addiction. Instead, she saw the good in me and thought I was amazing.

It was a revelation for me. I had always felt like I was damaged goods, even more so now than ever, but she showed me that I was capable of love and happiness. She opened her own damaged yet salvageable heart to me.

Together, we worked on building a new life for ourselves. We went to everywhere together, explored new hobbies, and talked about our dreams for the future. For the first time in a long time, I felt like I had something to live for. I feel happy.

Now, I'm proud to say that I'm still sober with help. I'm grateful every day for the woman who believed in me when I didn't believe in myself.

The first time I met her family, I was a bundle of nerves. I had heard so much about them, and I knew how important they were to her. I wanted to make a good impression, but I was also worried about whether they would accept me.

But from the moment I walked in the door, I felt welcomed. Her parents and Grandmother greeted me with open arms, and her brother and wife was friendly and kind. We all sat down to dinner together, and I felt like I was part of the family. We talked and laughed, and I was so grateful to be included in such a warm and loving group.

As the evening went on, I realised how happy it made me to feel accepted by her family. I had been in relationships before where I had felt like I had to hide, where I couldn't be my true self around the other person's family. But with her and her family, I felt like I could be completely honest and open. They didn't judge me or make me feel like an outsider. They saw me for who I was, and they liked me anyway.

I knew then that my she was the right person for me. She had brought me into her family, and they had embraced me with open hearts. It meant so much to me to feel like I was part of something bigger than just our relationship. I could see how much she loved her family, and how important they were to her. And now, they were important to me too.

Leaving her family that night, I felt a sense of happiness that I hadn't felt in a long time. I knew that there would be challenges ahead, but I also knew that I had a support system in place. I had her, and I had her family. And that was enough to make me feel like anything was possible.

Falling in love with the most amazing woman has been an experience unlike any other. I've never felt such intense emotions before, nor have I ever been so connected with another person on such a deep level. From the moment I met her, I knew there was something special about her.

We have so much in common, and our conversations flow effortlessly. I feel like I could talk to her for hours and never run out of things to say.

Falling in love, is a term that gets used far too familiarly.

As we got to know each other better, my feelings for her continued to grow. She was so kind and compassionate, and I could feel her genuine care and concern for me. I began to open up to her, sharing my quirks and past mistakes without fear of judgment. She listened with understanding and never once made me feel ashamed of who I was.

It was then that I realised how much I loved her. I loved the way she made me feel, the way she looked at me, and the way she accepted me for who I was. I felt like I had finally found someone who loved me unconditionally and that I could be myself around her.

Our love was passionate and emotional, and we were there for each other through thick and thin. We laughed together, cried together, and shared our dreams and aspirations. I knew that no matter what life through our way, we would always be there for each other.

Falling in love with her was a magical experience, and I cherished every moment we spent together. Whether we were sitting together on the couch or exploring new places, every moment is now special because we are together.

Falling in love with an amazing woman who loves you unconditionally is a transformative experience. It's an intense and emotional journey that leaves you feeling fulfilled and content. I will always cherish the memories and moments I share with her and will always be there for her no matter what life brings our way.

13. MY LOCAL ALCOHOL SERVICE IN THE COMMUNITY

Just to begin, I just want to point the difference between a service and a treatment centre, a service is a body of people commissioned in the local area for community treatment, a treatment centre is a rehabilitation centre. It's the services job to apply for the funding and placement at a rehabilitation centre.

I know it's sad, however the harsh realisation is the lack of professional support out there is horrendous. My personal experience has shown how it's a post-code lottery. That where you live determines if you're eligible for treatment.

Personally, in the service I use, one person is totally responsible for all funding applications., This one person gets to play god. They even told me, to my face. That they only submit applications where they know they'll get the funding., So it doesn't damage their professional reputation,

The whole system is corrupt. I think I met my care worker twice. All the other appointments that they missed. We're never revisited., How they could make judgements on my chaotic life when they clearly had their own issues going on.

I turned up to sessions and was the only user there.

I just feel like these services warehouse people for the funding from local councils.

I firmly believe there should be a well-managed national service to help anybody regardless of their postcode.

As I sit here reflecting on my experience with addiction treatment services, I can't help but feel incredibly let down.

When I first sought out help, I had high hopes for the services on offer. I was ready to make a change and committed to doing whatever it takes to overcome my addiction.

I remember walking into the building for the first time, feeling hopeful and optimistic. The staff members seemed friendly and professional, and the building was clean and well-maintained. But as time went on, my optimism quickly turned to disappointment.

The weekly sessions seemed to lack direction and focus. Instead of providing me with the tools and support I needed to overcome my addiction, I felt like I was just going through the motions. The staff members were often unresponsive and seemed disinterested in my progress. It was like they didn't really care about helping me.
As a result, I found myself becoming increasingly frustrated and disillusioned. My addiction began to take hold once again, and I felt like I was back where I started. The lack of support

and guidance from the service had a devastating impact on my recovery, and I struggled to maintain sobriety.

Looking back on my experience, I can't help but feel angry and let down. Addiction is a difficult and challenging disease, and it's essential that community services provide the support and resources necessary for recovery. Unfortunately, my local service I participated in failed to do so, and I suffered the consequences.

In conclusion, addiction treatment services are meant to provide individuals with the tools and support they need to overcome addiction. When they fall short, it can have a devastating impact on recovery. It's crucial that we hold treatment programs accountable and demand better resources and support for those struggling with addiction.

14. THE DISEASE CONCEPT

<u>Primary</u>

Understanding and reading the literature that's already out there and as I now grasp. Alcoholism is a disease of its own accord.

It is primary such as other chronic diseases like heart disease, liver failure and diabetes.

Later I will explore the genetic factors.

However, as I understand, my body and brain were predisposition due to my upbringing, environmental factors also the chemical imbalance of Tetrahydrolsoqulnoline

(THIQ) in my brain. I understand that being an alcoholic had left me to have low serotonin and dopamine levels. I have used alcohol to "up" these levels, until it become my worst enemy. Then lowering these levels, contributing to secondary issues.

Depression, Anxiety and feelings of being fundamentally unhappy. Leading to thoughts of suicide and an attempt of taking my own life.

When I crossed the "line" I even went as far as using cocaine to up the balance, which I was already trying but failing to balance with alcohol.

Although I never saw cocaine as an issue, it clearly was at the time. It was a mind a mind-altering substance. Which I knew I was using to try and find my balance,

I have only ever been able to find this balance with each step-in recovery, and sobriety.

Reading the literature, it makes me more determined not to "Pick up again"

I don't want a primary disease being the focal point of the causes of any more secondary issues.

I don't want to rely on mind altering substance to try and restore my balance.

I know there is contrary facts to the belief that Alcoholism is a disease. Many would suggest that Alcoholism is self-inflicted or you're just an ordinary typical heavy drinker.

However, if you read the studies and literature. There is evidence to the contrary which proves the disease concept. I also suggest that doubters look at Alcohol withdrawal from a neurology point of view rather than from just the physical symptoms. Studies into the angling effect have shown what happens to the brain when you detox too many times. This is why when you're discharged from a hospital with a view to carry on drinking. As with the angling affect, withdrawal can only get worst.

Progressive

As mentioned, if you look at the study by Virgina Davis, in an alcohol when they drink, toxic chemical is stored in the brain known as THIQ. This finally answers my question to why I never could never drink again.

The studies shows that certain kinds of rats would rather die of thirst than drink alcohol. However, when injected with minute quantities of THIC directly into the brain they would much rather pick alcohol, showing the THIC controls the requirement to consume alcohol.

As Virgina Davis expanded on this hypothesis, they repeated the test on our closest revolutionised cousins. Primates.

To conclude the test, they then kept these monkeys dry for seven years. Enough for all the cells in their body to regenerate. However, levels of THIC were still detected in the brain. Showing why the alcoholic can certainty never drink again.

Showing that no matter how many years you maybe in recovery, you'll always be in recovery, something which I personally I am always going to have to remind myself of. I will always be an alcoholic in recovery. I will never be recovered. I can just imagine it now though; it has ruined the idea of a chimp's tea party for me now. Knowing their having an AA meeting instead.

Joking aside, I know I'd rather be a sober monkey with seven years in recovery, rather than a Rataholic.

Just this I personally took as a huge metaphor and the realisation of how progressive this disease is.

Now I understand Alcoholism as a progressive disease I remember when I truly crossed the line. I'd ran away to Spain and drank heavily for 3 months. Only upon reflection have I realised the two days before I came home, I'd gone through my first delirium tremors. Rather than the flu as I'd previously thought and put it down to at the time.

Although for several years later I was unknowingly control drinking. I was in fact an alcoholic. Not just a boozy boyfriend, as my ex would have liked me to believe.

If \I continue to look at my own journey through alcoholism. I now see the early warning signs as I'd have foolishly put previous withdrawals in a denial stage.

"Oh, it was a heavy night." Or "Just the hair of the do will cure me."

Even so far as being told by people I truly care for "What makes you bad makes you better." Well thanks for that as I'm now learning about my disease in a rehabilitation centre. When all you wanted was for me to get my wallet out on a rough Sunday afternoon. However, you'll still have the same behaviours whilst I'm sat in serene recovery.

After I crossed that all so proverbial line and I accepted I was an Alcoholic. I look how it manifested within me and progressed.

When I started to hide my drinking, the bottles hidden around the house, the lies, deceit and betrayal. The number of miniatures bought from the shop for "Toothache"

Even down to having the staff rota on my phone, just so I wouldn't get severed by the same person twice.

Even when I admitted my problem to my ex-wife, that I was indeed an alcoholic, all she asked was I stopped hiding the amount I was drinking. All this did was enable me to drink more and openly without the guilt. This is where I was truly was powerless over alcohol and my life had become unmanageable. I often wondered as my disease progressed was there a point where I could have stopped?

However, as I now understand it as a progressive disease. The chemistry in my brain was telling me I wasn't an alcoholic so unless I'd have gotten help, I would have always been on the slippery slope. Even when I admitted to my disease, I was still relapsing showing just how progressive this disease is.

Chronic

As with other chronic diseases, it is same as with alcoholism. It is for life. I stupidly believed at some point I close this as just a chapter of my life and just live in recovery. However, I realise now, that I take my mind away from recovery and the programme, that the THIQ in my brain and without the right tools to live a sober life I could quite easily relapse. For years I survived in active addiction. Now I'm to live and achieve in active recovery. I look back in anguish at my own health problems, consequences of my addiction, that have arisen from my disease. If I look at my stroke two years ago, to now having a fatty liver, an enlarged spleen. Even going as far as projectile vomiting litres of bloods. To now being told I'm extremely close to blowing a verisese. If I continue drinking. Knowing if that I do blow a vericise it' major surgery or worst die from blood loss itself.

I have learnt a great deal about my disease within the first few days of an inpatient rehabilitation programme. Especially with the whys and what ifs?

One questions I have explored is; if they were to invent a pill and miracle cure, would I take it and return to social drinking? I wouldn't as I believe some of the challenges and personal battles I have faced and fought have shaped me, my story and my truth. Also have created who I am today. Which is better than I ever could have imagined.

Even now in Rehabilitation, after I decided to stop shrinking myself and be more me than I have ever been. I'm well-liked by my peers, even more so than if I would have shrunken myself and was to act like someone who I'm not. So, no I wouldn't take a miracle cure. I'm a chronic alcoholic with still a big personality and a lot of love to give.

Knowing now the disease is both progressive and chronic, any form of relapse can only make things worse. As with the Angling Affect. I couldn't imagine what form any kind of relapse would take. Just by learning these facts and researching this information has scared the living hell out of me.

Already at this point I don't want to ever drink again. Yet playing another tape forward but more informed has only concreted this knowledge within me.

Unlike some other chronic diseases, alcoholism is progressive. I will continue to remind myself of this in my recovery.

Just because I may face triggers later in my life, I now must use my time in rehab to learn alternative methods and skills to deal with these instead of pushing the fuck it button.,

As that's will always be stored withing the THIQ in my brain. This chemical reminds me often of the prominent presence of this button.

Pressing this ever, will only be determent to my recover, nobody I know ever had a good relapse anyway.

I never chose to become an alcoholic. Who would choose? Would you? The sweats, the shakes, the incontinence, the nightmares even the blackouts!

Genetics

It is commonly explored that genetics, can cause you to have a predisposition to becoming an alcoholic, that alcoholism is heredity, there are members of my extended family both in recovery and addiction.

Although I did explore this in Rehab, it is personal to them and for their anonymity I wouldn't comment on another person's journey.

Looking at the genetic factor, it is proven that you are four times more likely to become an addict if there is a member of your family suffering from addiction.

Fatal

Fatal, it is what it is! Fatality is the result of this progressive and chronic disease. It ends with death.

Upon reflection I look at my health issues and I must take a long look at myself. Knowing I could easily blow a vericise, easily translates to one drink could kill me.

As I have progressed in my disease, I know I can't just have one drink. This reminds me of an old proverb. One is too many and a thousand is never enough., I also must look on what affect the kindling affect has had on my body and neurology,

I remember just how horrendous and unfortunately graphic my last detox was. I couldn't breathe. I couldn't move, I was waiting for death. I didn't see medicine helping. I truly believed that I was going to die. There's a line from a song. It goes; "If I die young, bury me in satin, lay me down on a bed of roses, pray for my mother as she buries her baby"

As I write this with a sober mind, I couldn't imagine anything worst that me losing my fight with my addiction and the pain it which it would cause. I couldn't imagine this playing the tape forward. Just proves well to me anyways. I know the ultimate end of the progression of this disease is eventual death.

There has been a time whilst in active addiction I took an attempt on my own life. Purely from the secondary effects of this primary disease. I don't want to die.

I am determined now more than ever to keep taking that next step.

I lost a close and friend a little while ago, he was a covert alcoholic. We all knew really, but never said anything. I look back and wonder if he had recovery and a programme if he would still be with us? Or how many people there are in the world of addiction trying to get help but can't, or in some cases just won't.

To summarise, this is a disease, it is primary, it's a disease of its own accord, not cause by any secondary factors. It is a progressive disease from which only gets worst from when THIQ is present in the brain. There is no cure. You will always be in recovery.

You'll never been able to stop, or it will keep progressing.

One factor which can contribute to the alcoholic is genetics and the predispositions were exposed to as infants.

It is a chronic illness where you need to be able to work a

programme.

Ignoring all this can only result in one certain way; it being fatal.

This disease kills.

I will not let this disease kill me.

I'm worth more.

THANK YOU, READERS,

Dear Readers,

I just want to express my deepest gratitude to each and every one of you who has read my book on recovery from alcoholism, domestic abuse, trauma, and heartbreak.

Your support and encouragement have meant the world to me, and I am truly humbled by the impact that my words have had on your lives.

When I first set out to write this book, it was with the intention of sharing my own story of pain and triumph in the hopes that it might resonate with even one person. And to hear from so many of you that it has done just that, fills me with a sense of joy and purpose that I cannot adequately express in words.

To know that my experiences and struggles have helped you feel less alone, less ashamed, less helpless, means everything to me. If my book has given even one person the strength to seek help, the courage to leave an abusive relationship, or the hope to believe that recovery is possible, then I feel that I have succeeded in my mission.

Your messages of support and feedback have touched me deeply, and I want you to know that each one is read with care and consideration.

Your stories of resilience and strength inspire me to keep writing and to keep sharing my own journey with honesty and vulnerability.

Thank you from the bottom of my heart for taking the time to read my words, and for allowing me to be a small part of your own journey towards healing and self-discovery.
With love and gratitude,

Kieran

X

WHATS NEXT?

The Journey has only just begun, This has been my journey through recovery, However this has been about how I survived the Devil's grip on me. How I am alive, clean, serene to share the harrowing truth of addiction.

I am currently collaborating with another author. We're looking at alternative methods of recovery, How I used a combined recovery method tailored for me, Recovery should be focused on induvial alone, It's not a one fits all method.,

I personally couldn't rely on AA alone., or SMART Recovery, I've used Therapy, Counselling and strength-based exercises to start me on my journey,

I am also working on a fiction novel. Based loosely on some of the exciting people I have met on my recovery journey.

FINAL NOTE

There is no way I couldn't share this experience with you. The night I finished writing this book, I was in a cabin, in the middle of nowhere taking advantage of an opportunity to focus. The weather had been horrible my entire stay. As soon as I finished typing my final words, I stepped outside, Following old habits I looked to the sky. All I could see was hundreds of stars shining away, being from the city I don't think I've ever seen so many starts in sky at once,

Not only that a song from my favourite musical was playing., I stepped out to the words

So, if you care to find me, Look to the western sky, as someone told me lately "Everyone deserves the chance to fly" I'm defying gravity and you won't bring me down"

What a wonderful experience.

SERVICES THAT CAN HELP

In An Emergency Phone 999

Alcoholic Anonymous
www.alcoholics-anonymous.org.uk
0800 9177 650
help@aamail.org

Talk to Frank
www.talktofrank.com
0300 1236600

The Samaritans
www.samaritans.org
116 123

Don't suffer in silence. Reach out

ABOUT THE AUTHOR

Kieran was born and raised in Manchester, UK, after education Kieran pursued a career in the public sector, specifically public transport., Eventually leading him to join law. He took some time out to run Public Houses, after he realised, he had an addiction he sought care in the community, which was unhelpful, he managed to enter rehab, where he wrote this book.
He comes from a loving family of a Mother, Father, Stepfather, Sister & Partner and Two stepbrothers.
He loves animals especially Kobe and Rory. His dogs. In his spare time Kieran enjoys endless impulsive decisions, tinkering and now writing.

Kieran has written this book during Rehab and afterwards. Spending time in Slaverly UK, The cabin in the woods now that holds the memories he no longer needs to look back on.

If you would like to get in contact with the author, you can do so at
contact@survivor-book.com
Or you can visit
www.survivor-book.com

Kieran would be happy to attend for readings, signings, Q&A's and motivational speaking.

Let the community live on at
www.facebook.com/survivor.book

Printed in Great Britain
by Amazon